Weekends for Two in the

MID-ATLANTIC STATES

50 ROMANTIC GETAWAYS

BY BILL GLEESON

PHOTOGRAPHS BY CARY HAZLEGROVE

CHRONICLE BOOKS

SAN FRANCISCO

CONTENTS

❧

The photographer wishes to
thank the following people
for their assistance, inspiration
and support:

Macy Cassin
Anne Butler
Amanda Martin
Dan Rudder

Printed in Hong Kong.

Library of Congress
Cataloging-in-Publication
Data available.

ISBN 0-8118-1608-7

Design: Poulson/Gluck Design

Distributed in Canada
by Raincoast Books,
8680 Cambie Street
Vancouver, B.C.
V6P 6M9

10 9 8 7 6 5 4 3 2 1

Chronicle Books
85 Second Street
San Francisco, CA 94105

www.chroniclebooks.com

INTRODUCTION

For some, the inspiration to write a book might come during a walk in the woods or while staring at a sunset. Our muse visited us in a funky bedroom in Napa, California.

It was on a crisp fall harvest weekend a number of years ago that the two of us ventured blissfully away from work and children for what we hoped would be a quiet romantic weekend. Unfortunately, the quaint "country bed-and-breakfast inn" that the brochure promised turned out to be a drab, suburban family home whose empty-nester owners were renting out their children's rooms to make a few extra dollars. The kids' clothes still hung in our bedroom closet, and the tacky "art" on the walls was literally priced to sell.

Although the weekend didn't match our expectations, it did inspire us. In 1990 we hit the road in a quest to separate romantic fact from fiction and to hopefully spare other couples similar disappointment. Thus began a coast-to-coast pilgrimage that has since taken us through more than a dozen states in search of the nation's most romantic destinations.

Along the way we've experienced the getaway gamut, from seductively sublime to downright somber and seedy. We've also been able to refine our romantic scorecard.

ROOMS FOR ROMANCE

While few destinations described in the following pages are equipped with all of the romantic touches listed below, each offers at least a few. Our romantic criteria include:

- In-room fireplaces

- Tubs and showers big enough for two

- Breakfast in the privacy of your room

- Couches or love seats

- Canopied, four-poster, king-sized beds with romantic dressings

- Private decks, patios, or balconies with inspirational views

- Special touches such as ultrasensuous European-style comforters, extra-cushy towels, bathrobes, wine or champagne, chocolates, fruit, mood lighting, stereos, and fresh flowers

Finally, we're partial to those establishments where privacy is ensured, where the innkeeper isn't always underfoot, where interior walls are well insulated, and where child guests are discouraged. While we certainly harbor no prejudice toward children—we have two of our own—many couples are seeking a well-deserved break from the kids. The (sometimes loud) evidence of little people in the room next door or in the hall doesn't exactly contribute to a passionate getaway.

CHOOSING A ROMANTIC ROOM

Many guidebooks are so lavish in their descriptions of lobbies, libraries, and parlors, you wonder whether the authors have even set foot inside a guest room. We've elected to focus our descriptions on specific guest rooms that offer the best romantic amenities. After all, we know where you're going to spend most of your time during that special getaway. It's certainly not the lobby.

When calling for a reservation, instead of leaving the choice of rooms to the innkeeper, don't hesitate to ask about the availability of a particularly appealing room we've described—unless, of course, you already have a personal favorite. Although some innkeepers won't guarantee a specific room, most will attempt to honor your request.

A WORD ABOUT RATES

While most savvy travelers can still find a room along the interstate for less than $50, this isn't a bargain hunter's book. Since romantic getaways are occasions to cherish, you'll need to adjust to the higher tariffs being commanded for these special places. Most of the choicest rooms described in the following pages start at more than $100 per night.

To help you plan your getaway budget, approximate 1999 rates for specific rooms are noted within and at the end of each description. Keep in mind that rates are subject to change without notice. We strongly suggest that you check the rates before making a reservation. Also keep in mind that an increasing number of establishments require two-night minimum stays on weekends and holidays, so plan your budget accordingly.

Peak-season (circa 1999) room rates for a Friday or Saturday night for two people are classified in the following ranges, not including tax:

> Moderate: Under $150
>
> Expensive: $150–$199
>
> Deluxe: $200 or more

FINAL NOTES

No payment was sought or accepted from any establishment in exchange for a listing in this book.

Food, wine, and flowers were occasionally added to photos for styling purposes. Some establishments offer such amenities; others do not. If these touches are important to you, please ask at the time you make a reservation whether they're complimentary or whether they're provided for an extra charge. Also, please understand that we cannot guarantee that inns will maintain furnishings or standards as they existed on our visit. We appreciate hearing from readers if their experience is at variance with our description. Reader comments are carefully consulted in the creation and revision of each *Weekends for Two* volume. See the form near the back of the book for our address and our free romantic travel offer.

Virginia

Daytime Diversions

In Charlottesville, the enchanting Thomas Jefferson–designed "academic village" of the University of Virginia is worth a self-guided tour.

Plan on spending at least a half day if you visit Jefferson's estate, Monticello, located about two miles outside Charlottesville. Buses transport visitors from the parking area up Jefferson's "little mountain" to the estate proper, where informative tours of the Palladian house, grounds, and gardens are offered.

Williamsburg is a historic eighteenth-century community that includes more than five hundred public buildings, homes, stores, and taverns. There is a fee for access to many buildings and for guided tours. Throughout the colonial settlement, visitors encounter costumed tradespeople and character actors. Be sure to cover the less-traveled side streets and stroll through Williamsburg's romantic gardens.

The Shenandoah Apple Blossom Festival is held in Winchester each spring. Northern Virginia is home to a number of wineries.

The Chrysler Museum in Norfolk was rated by the *Wall Street Journal* as one of the top twenty art museums in the United States. Also in Norfolk is the Waterside Festival Marketplace with nearly a hundred shops, restaurants, and clubs. You can tour Norfolk's historic harbor aboard a topsail schooner or a paddle wheeler.

Tables for Two

In Norfolk, Ship's Cabin on East Ocean View overlooks Chesapeake Bay, while Freemason Abbey on West Freemason Street offers a dining experience within the walls of a century-old church.

The Trellis in Merchant Square is our innkeepers' choice in Colonial Williamsburg.

Visitors to Richmond who are interested in regional cuisine should try Millie's Restaurant on East Main Street or the Frog & the Redneck on East Cary Street in Shockoe Slip near the financial district.

In Charlottesville, try the "new American" cuisine of Metropolitain on Water Street or the fixed-price dinners at Clifton— The Country Inn (see listing in this section). A dinner at the Inn at Little Washington is reason alone to travel to the quaint community of Washington (see listing in this section). Highly rated five-course meals are served to guests of and visitors to L'Auberge Provençale in White Post (see listing in this section).

PAGE HOUSE INN

323 Fairfax Avenue
Norfolk, VA 23507
Telephone: (804) 625-5033; toll-free: (800) 599-7659

Six bedrooms, each with private bath; three with
fireplaces; one with tub for two. Complimentary
continental breakfast served at communal table, tables for
two, or in your room. No handicapped access. Smoking
is not permitted. Two-night minimum stay required April
through October; two- or three-night minimum during
holiday periods. Moderate to expensive.

Getting There
From Interstate 264, take exit 9 onto Waterside Drive.
Continue approximately one mile to Olney Road. Turn
left and drive two blocks to Mowbray Arch. Turn left and
drive one block to Fairfax Avenue. Turn right; inn is first
building on the left.

PAGE HOUSE INN ✍ Norfolk

About a century ago, a new Norfolk suburb called Ghent was born a few blocks west of the city's commercial hub. Herman Page, the real estate man who planned the upscale neighborhood, built the two-and-a-half-story Georgian Revival home now known as the Page House Inn.

When innkeepers Stephanie and Ezio DiBelardino arrived on the scene in 1990, the structure was a "boarded-up, rotting hulk" that some locals wanted demolished. A former business development executive, Stephanie worked successfully to overcome a Norfolk ordinance prohibiting bed-and-breakfast inns, while Ezio, a master craftsman, skillfully renovated the structure. His thoughtful touches include rich oak woodwork, contemporary plumbing, door locks, and soundproofing in the walls and between floors. All rooms have televisions, telephones, and clock radios.

ROOMS FOR ROMANCE

Arguably the most romantic room in the house is the Bathe Suite (high $100 range), which takes its name from the sumptuous bathroom that's nearly as big as the bedroom. Features include a huge sunken tub for two with built-in lounge seats, a combination shower and steam room for two, a bidet, a European-style commode, and a double vanity.

Mistress Adella's Suite (mid $100 range) offers a queen-sized canopied bed, a gas log fireplace, a chaise longue, and a sitting room with a bay window. There's also a spa tub for one.

Decorated in handsome deep green and burgundy hues, Mr. Herman's Room (low $100 range) holds a black walnut canopied bed, a gas fireplace, and a spa tub for two.

Miss Diane's Suite (mid $100 range), which overlooks the Chrysler Museum, is the inn's most expensive accommodation. It has gas log fireplaces in both the sitting room and the bedroom, a private dining room in which the two of you may enjoy breakfast, a queen-sized white iron bed, and a restored clawfoot tub with shower.

Miss Hulda's Room (around $100) has a queen-sized mahogany sleigh bed and a bathroom in the eaves that features a restored four-foot-long clawfoot tub with shower as well as a love seat.

LIBERTY ROSE
BED-AND-BREAKFAST INN

1022 Jamestown Road
Williamsburg, VA 23185
Telephone: (757) 253-1260

Four rooms, each with private bath; one with fireplace;
one with tub for two. Complimentary full breakfast
served at tables for two. No handicapped access.
Smoking is not permitted. Two-night minimum stay
required during weekends; three-night minimum during
holiday periods. Moderate to expensive.

Getting There
From Interstate 64, take exit 242A. Continue five miles to
Jamestown Road. Turn right; inn is one-half mile on a hill
on the left.

LIBERTY ROSE
BED-AND-BREAKFAST INN ✤ Williamsburg

Soft lights illuminating the four little dormers caught our eye as we drove along Jamestown Road after a splendid day of Virginia sightseeing. Set under tall trees atop a gentle hill, Liberty Rose is a picture-perfect destination in a classically beautiful community.

While many innkeepers we meet have an eye toward expansion, Liberty Rose proprietors Brad and Sandra Hirz are happy with the four guest rooms that comprise their 1920s-era home-turned-inn. This enchanting bed-and-breakfast inn may be our smallest recommended Mid-Atlantic destination, but it's big on romance and luxury. Like they say, good things come in small packages.

ROOMS FOR ROMANCE

Like each of the inn's three other rooms, Rose Victoria (around $200) is lavished with attention to detail. The room's centerpiece is an elegant fringed and tassled queen-sized bed angled against a wall covered in deep red damask. Not to be outdone, the large bathroom contains a stunning oak wall taken from an old rowhouse, an oversized antique tub, and a red marble shower. This is the only guest room on the first floor.

Magnolia's Peach (high $100 range), where we spent a cozy summer night, is a study in tasteful Victorian decor. Antique prints, lamps, pillows, fresh and faux flowers, doilies, and collectibles are artfully arranged, and a queen-sized carved poster bed is canopied with embroidered lace. The small bathroom holds a pedestal sink and an oversized black tiled shower.

Six windows illuminate Suite Williamsburg (around $200), furnished with a grand carved queen-sized bed draped in silk and jacquard fabric. This room, fit for a honeymoon, has a working fireplace and a sitting area. Entering the bathroom through stained-glass doors, you'll find a black marble shower and a clawfoot tub, as well as porcelain candelabras.

The smallest room is Savannah Lace (low to mid $100 range), equipped with antiques, a tall queen-sized poster bed, and a bath with a dormer window and an antique clawfoot tub. This room doesn't have a shower.

Rooms here have televisions and videocassette players that are hidden in unusual places, like an antique birdcage and a doll "mansion."

LINDEN ROW INN

100 East Franklin Street
Richmond, VA 23219
Telephone: (804) 783-7000

Seventy rooms, each with private bath. Complimentary
continental breakfast is served in the inn's restaurant.
Communal spa. Handicapped access. Smoking is
allowed. Moderate to expensive.

Getting There
From north Interstate 95 or west Interstate 64, take exit
76B. Turn left on Leigh Street, right on Belvidere Street,
left on Franklin Street, left on Second Street, left on
Grace Street, and left on First Street. From south
Interstate 95, take exit 74A onto 195 Downtown
Expressway, and exit at Canal Street. Turn right at
Second Street, left on Grace Street, and left on First
Street. The inn is on the left at First and Franklin Streets.

LINDEN ROW INN ❧ Richmond

According to local legend, the nineteenth-century garden that's now the courtyard centerpiece of Linden Row Inn inspired Edgar Allan Poe's love poem, "To Helen." Whether or not this lovely spot was the source of Poe's romantic inspiration will probably forever remain a mystery, but Linden Row is definitely igniting sparks among visitors today.

These Greek Revival–style townhouses, part of an eclectic historic neighborhood whose gentrification was still in progress at the time of our visit, boast their original handsome red-brick facades, gleaming white-columned porches, and tall shuttered windows. Separated by wrought-iron fencing, the structures still appear from the street to be a series of separate residences. However, they're interconnected at the rear by walkways, hallways, and stairways.

ROOMS FOR ROMANCE

Built more than 150 years ago, the complex offers a total of seventy refurbished and restored rooms. Guests of Linden Row Inn may choose either a garden room or one of the main house rooms.

Typical of the garden accommodations, room 132 (around $100) is moderately sized with carpeting, a double bed, one chair, a luggage armoire, a small writing desk, and a decorative brick fireplace. This first-floor room faces the lawn and courtyard area.

For a more memorable romantic getaway, we recommend a room or a suite in the main house facing Franklin Street and a large old magnolia tree. We were very impressed with room 216 (mid $100 range), a high-ceilinged second-floor Parlor Suite. In the sitting room, a burgundy antique love seat and matching armchairs are arranged under an ornate chandelier and next to a decorative marble fireplace. A tall antique mirror is flanked by floor-to-ceiling windows draped in burgundy.

Separated from the sitting room by two massive sliding doors, the large bedroom holds a queen-sized bed, a beautiful burled antique bureau, a second decorative fireplace, and an armoire that conceals a television. The ample bathroom has a tub-and-shower combination.

PROSPECT HILL PLANTATION INN

2887 Poindexter Road
Trevilians, VA 23093
Telephone toll-free: (800) 277-0844

Thirteen rooms, each with private bath, some with fireplace;
seven with tubs for two. Complimentary full breakfast served
at tables for two or in your room. Rates include dinner for
two. Swimming pool and restaurant. No handicapped access.
Smoking is allowed. Two-night minimum stay required during
weekends; two- to three-night minimum during holiday
periods. Deluxe.

Getting There

The inn is fifteen miles east of Charlottesville. From eastbound
Interstate 64, take exit 136 and turn right on Route 15 south,
and drive a quarter mile to Zion Crossroads. At stop light,
turn left onto Route 250 east and drive one mile to Route 613
on left. Follow Route 613 for three miles to inn on left.

PROSPECT HILL
PLANTATION INN ✍ Trevilians

W hen Captain William Overton returned to his plantation near Charlottesville after the Civil War, he found his fields overgrown and most of the slave quarters abandoned. Over the next several years his family changed the focus of the property and began receiving guests, expanding the sixteenth-century main house and renovating the small slave cabins that surrounded it.

A little more than a century later, the current owners, the Sheehan family, rehabilitated the compound and in the process created one of the most unusual and, in our opinion, romantic inns in Virginia.

It's only a few minutes from Charlottesville and Monticello, but the plantation is situated well off the beaten path at the end of a narrow lane in the foothills. Rare magnolias and tall tulip poplars shade the property, and expansive lawn areas help create a serene and peaceful atmosphere.

ROOMS FOR ROMANCE

The two-story, yellow-and-white manor house contains many romantic accommodations, some of which have fireplaces. However, the little cottages that surround the main house are what set this property apart from other fine country inns we've visited. For a romantic experience you'll not soon forget, we suggest the two of you try one of the cabins. You won't be sorry. In addition, all the room rates noted here include dinner for two in the inn's restaurant.

One of our favorites is the Overseer's Cottage (mid $300 range), a two-room hideaway located near the swimming pool. In the bedroom, a four-poster bed is set beneath a window and faces two wing chairs and a fireplace. You step down through French doors to a charming multiwindowed sitting room with chairs and a table. The tiled bathroom has three windows and a spa tub into which the two of you might be able to squeeze. The cottage also has its own small porch.

Sanco Pansy's (mid $300 range), a remote cottage set at the rear of the compound behind tall bushes, is the honeymooners' choice. The cottage has a front porch with a sweeping view. Inside is a tiny step-down sitting room with a wicker couch. The large bedroom is decorated in chintz fabrics, is furnished with a wicker love seat, and has a handsome brick fireplace. A step-down bathroom has a deep spa tub with a shower head.

Entering the Boy's Cabin (around $300), with its brick floor and authentic log walls with white chinking, is like stepping back in time. The eerie ambience we initially felt upon entering the dark and primitive little cabin soon gave way to a cozy romantic feeling, especially after we saw the large bathroom with its tiled floor and spa tub. This is the plantation's most unusual accommodation.

A good choice during the winter months is the Summer Kitchen (lower $300 range), whose convenient location near the main house means you'll not have to venture far for meals. Inside is a wing chair, a rocker, and a fireplace with a large brick hearth. The tiled bathroom, whose picture window overlooks a sweeping lawn and the treetops of a distant valley, has a deep spa tub that might hold two in a pinch.

KESWICK HALL

701 Club Drive

Keswick, VA 22947

Telephone: (804) 979-3440; toll-free: (800) 274-5391

Forty-eight rooms, each with private bath. Complimentary full breakfast served in the inn's restaurant or in your room. Golf course, tennis courts, game room, indoor and outdoor swimming pools, and spa facilities. Handicapped access. Smoking is allowed. Deluxe.

Getting There

From westbound Interstate 64 from Richmond, take the Keswick/Boyds Tavern exit. Turn right on Route 616 and drive three-tenths of a mile to Keswick Estate security entrance on left.

KESWICK HALL ❧ Keswick

"Here, in Jefferson's cradle of American architecture, we wanted to create a community where traditional houses in spacious surroundings are in harmony with an unspoiled countryside of woods and walks and views," said Sir Bernard Ashley, who along with his late wife, the famed decorator Laura Ashley, acquired and developed the six-hundred-acre Keswick Estate in the hills not far from Monticello and Charlottesville.

To help showcase the development, the Ashleys built a grand country house hotel called Keswick Hall, which presides over a gated, exclusive community of large homes, an Arnold Palmer–designed golf course, indoor and outdoor swimming pools, and a fitness center.

Part of the Ashley House Hotels (there are two other properties), Keswick Hall is a comfortable but formal destination where English afternoon tea and scones are served in the parlor rooms and where guests may enjoy a game of snooker after dinner. Meals are served in a large dining room on the lower level. At the time of our visit, fixed-price dinners were offered for around $60 per person; a full breakfast is included in the room rate.

ROOMS FOR ROMANCE

As you might expect, Keswick Hall features Laura Ashley fabrics and wall coverings, and each guest room is furnished with fine antiques and art. Room 27 (mid $500 range), our very large room for a special summer night, holds a handsome canopied king-sized bed, a love seat, and an antique writing desk. The spacious, bright, white tiled bathroom has a long soaking tub big enough for two, a separate shower, and a towel warmer.

While the indoor environment left us wanting for nothing, our favorite feature was the large private deck, where we sat in wicker chairs and savored the seemingly endless treetop and Blue Ridge Mountain view beyond the fairways.

Smaller, elegantly appointed rooms without decks are available in the low $200 range. Rates for a larger and more lavish suite can climb as high as the mid $600 range.

CLIFTON—THE COUNTRY INN

1296 Clifton Inn Drive

Charlottesville, VA 22911

Telephone: (804) 971-1800; toll-free: (888) 971-1800

Fourteen rooms, each with private bath and woodburning
fireplace; one with tub for two. Complimentary full
breakfast served in the inn's restaurant. Swimming pool
and tennis courts. Handicapped access. Smoking is not
permitted. Two-night minimum stay required during
weekends. Expensive to deluxe.

Getting There

From Interstate 64 near Charlottesville, take exit 124.
Continue east on Highway 250. Turn right on Route 729
south. The inn is the second drive on the left.

CLIFTON—THE COUNTRY INN ✍ Charlottesville

The University of Virginia and Monticello aren't the only Charlottesville edifices bearing the Jefferson imprint. This magnificent mansion was built by Thomas Jefferson's daughter, Martha, and her husband, Thomas Mann Randolph, on land that was once part of Shadwell Plantation, Jefferson's birthplace.

Clifton is two centuries old and is listed on the National Register of Historic Places, but don't come for a visit expecting a musty shrine. With fireplaces in every room, a swimming pool and spa, downy comforters, a tennis court, and memorable meals, Clifton offers the kind of contemporary and romantic pleasures that could keep the two of you captivated for a week. Other attractions of this forty-acre property are a lake for swimming, fishing, and inner-tubing; a croquet lawn; and woodlands criss-crossed with nature trails.

Well known for its dining room, Clifton serves fixed-price dinners Wednesday through Saturday. On weekdays, plan on spending around $60 per person. Saturday dinners, which include additional courses, are slightly more expensive.

ROOMS FOR ROMANCE

A lavishly draped queen-sized bed is the centerpiece of room 4, the Martha Jefferson Room (mid to upper $200 range) on the second floor of the main house. A fireplace flickers at one side of the bed, and a semicircular couch offers romantic seating for two. The bath has a tub-and-shower combination and a pedestal sink.

We were intrigued with the long soaking tub for two and the tiled shower with four spigots found in the bathroom of room 2, the Thomas Mann Randolph Room (mid to upper $200 range), a front-facing second-floor room with a queen-sized bed, two cushy chairs, and a love seat.

Room 5 (high $200 range), called the Rivanna Room, is a three-room main house suite with a large sitting room where a bay window seat overlooks the garden and croquet lawn. The bathroom is large and sunny, and is equipped with a chaise longue, an old-fashioned soaking tub, a marble shower, and a dressing table. The corner bedroom holds a queen-sized bed and a fireplace.

Offered in the low $300 range is Clifton's most expensive accommodation: the luxurious suite in what was once the estate's carriage house. On the main level is a living room with hardwood floors and painted walls; it's furnished with a couch and chair and a baby grand piano and has a fireplace. Up a short stairway is a dormered sleeping loft with a queen-sized bed. The bathroom holds a tiled shower with double spigots and his and hers pedestal sinks. Artifacts from the home of American explorer Meriwether Lewis are also found in this room.

Guests may also spend a night in Thomas Mann Randolph's former law offices, which overlook the Rivanna River.

HIGH MEADOWS INN

High Meadows Lane (Route 4, Box 6)
Scottsville, VA 24590-9706
Telephone: (804) 286-2218; toll-free: (800) 232-1832

Fourteen rooms, each with private bath; twelve with
fireplaces, two with woodstoves; five with tubs for two.
Complimentary full breakfast served at tables for two or
in your room; rates include dinner for two. Restaurant.
Handicapped access. Smoking is not permitted. Two-
night minimum stay required during spring and fall
weekends and all holiday periods. Moderate to expensive.

Getting There
From Interstate 64 near Charlottesville, take exit 121
south. Follow State Highway 20 south for seventeen
miles. After crossing James River Road (Route 726),
continue three-tenths of a mile and turn left on High
Meadows Lane.

HIGH MEADOWS INN 🥀 Scottsville

igh Meadows Inn's centerpiece, a gracious old home referred to as the Vineyard Inn building, is certainly a comfortable place to spend the night; we'd recommend it to anyone who enjoys a bed-and-breakfast experience. As we toured it, however, we felt the Vineyard Inn building simply didn't distinguish itself as one of the Mid-Atlantic's fifty most romantic getaways. Then, just as we were about to press on to the next stop on our itinerary, our inn guide asked if we'd like to see the other accommodations that comprise High Meadows Inn. What we saw changed our minds.

Like Prospect Hill Plantation Inn (see previous listing), this property consists of multiple separate and distinct lodgings spread over several acres. Rates noted below are for a Saturday night stay and include dinner for two.

ROOMS FOR ROMANCE

In the Vineyard Inn building, we recommend the Music Room (low $200 range), located just off the entryway. This sunny corner tempts guests with a bay window, a working fireplace, a carved dark wood queen-sized bed, and a rose-colored in-room spa tub for two.

A short walk from the main house is the Carriage House, a contemporary addition that holds two delightfully romantic rooms. In the French Country Carriage House (mid $200 range), a round bed sits on a deep blue carpet under skylights. This room also has a fireplace, a kitchenette, and a spa for two on a private outdoor deck overlooking a wooded area.

Next door in the same building is the Cedar Carriage House (around $200), which has a queen-sized bed, a fireplace, and vaulted ceiling.

Glenside (mid $200 range) is a very private freestanding cottage decorated with a narrative wall mural. This eclectic and funky cottage has a living room with a couch and an easy chair, a kitchenette, and a bedroom with a queen-sized bed, a fireplace, and a love seat. The bathroom has a tub-and-shower combination.

Mountain Sunset, once a neighboring home, is now part of the High Meadows property. Inside the charming old residence is the luscious Cabernet 'n Creme suite (mid $200 range), equipped with a queen-sized canopied bed and a seven-foot-long English ivory soaking tub set by a fireplace. The suite also has a sun porch.

THE SAMPSON EAGON INN

238 E. Beverley Street
Staunton, VA 24401
Telephone: (540) 886-8200; toll-free: (800) 597-9722

Five rooms, each with private bath. Complimentary full breakfast served at a large communal table or a table for two or four. No handicapped access. Smoking is not permitted. Moderate.

Getting There

From Interstate 81, take exit 225 or exit 222 and follow the signs to Woodrow Wilson's birthplace. The inn is across the street from the birthplace museum at the corner of E. Beverley and Coalter Streets.

THE SAMPSON EAGON INN ❧ Staunton

We can attest from years of travel experiences that America is brimming with tacky old homes-turned-inns offering service as stale as the surroundings. Innkeepers of these types of establishments who wonder why they've still got empty rooms on Valentine's Day or why guests don't ever pay a return visit would be well served by a lesson or two from Frank and Laura Mattingly, whose Sampson Eagon Inn is a textbook example of how to turn a graceful historic residence into a romantic inn of distinction.

Situated in a well-kept neighborhood of impressive homes, including the birthplace of President Woodrow Wilson, the Sampson Eagon House opened as an inn in the early 1990s after two years of extensive refurbishing. "We know that the aura of nostalgia fades quickly when your antique bed fails to give you a good night's rest and your shower runs out of hot water," said Laura. Balancing history with romantic comfort in this two-hundred-year-old manor, they enlarged the antique beds to luscious canopied queens, created comfortable sitting areas for two, and added romantic lighting, luxurious linens, plush carpet, and contemporary bathrooms. There are additional niceties such as televisions and videocassette players in all the rooms, and the inn serves a memorable full breakfast.

ROOMS FOR ROMANCE

Their enticing suites were offered at the time of our visit for just a little over $100 per night, making the Sampson Eagon Inn a perfect choice for traveling romantics on a budget. The Eagon Suite and the Tams Suite (low $100 range), both occupying corners of the second floor, are our two favorites. In the Eagon Suite, a charming antique love seat sits at the foot of a handsome bed. The large bathroom contains two leaded-glass windows, a tub-and-shower combination, and extensive original wall cabinetry. There are also two comfortable chairs.

Guests enter the Tams Suite through a sitting room furnished with an antique writing desk and a daybed. The nicely windowed bedroom contains a love seat and a picture-perfect queen-sized bed with a bowed canopy. The bathroom has a tub-and-shower combination. The Eagon Suite has a decorative fireplace.

In the Kayser Room on the first floor, a crystal chandelier hangs above a canopied queen-sized bed and a love seat. Kitty's Room, a front-facing second-floor corner room, has a partially canopied brass bed, while the Holt Room, decorated in hues of blue and white, has a canopied bed and a matching contemporary love seat. These three rooms are offered for around $100.

THE INN AT LITTLE WASHINGTON
Middle and Main Streets (P.O. Box 300)
Washington, VA 22747
Telephone: (540) 675-3800

Fourteen rooms, each with private bath. Complimentary continental breakfast served in the inn's restaurant or in your room. Afternoon tea served daily. No handicapped access. Smoking is allowed in some public rooms. Deluxe.

Getting There
From Interstate 66 take exit 43-A. Follow Highway 29 south for twelve miles to Warrenton. In Warrenton, take Highway 211 west. Continue for twenty-three miles and turn right on Highway 211 Business to Washington. The inn is one-half mile on the right.

THE INN AT LITTLE WASHINGTON ✍ Washington

Wanting to see as much of this renowned property as possible, we wisely dropped by on a day when the guest rooms of the Inn at Little Washington were closed for cleaning and decorating. Otherwise, all we would have seen would have been locked doors hung with "do not disturb" signs.

Our hands-down choice for the Mid-Atlantic region's most romantic destination, the Inn at Little Washington rates a perfect on our scorecard. Even if you have to beg, borrow, or steal, try to savor a meal and an overnight stay here—it's a must for couples who enjoy good food, great accommodations, and each other.

A drive of about an hour and a half from Washington, D.C., the little burg of Washington was surveyed more than two and a half centuries ago by George Washington. The inn is situated on the town's only intersection. The acclaimed dining room, which serves multi-course, fixed-price meals, comprises the ground floor.

ROOMS FOR ROMANCE

We had read wonderful reviews of the inn's dinners, but the food critics were apparently too stuffed to make it upstairs to visit guest rooms. We were taken aback by the wonderfully exotic accommodations that await overnight guests here.

The guest rooms were described by one member of the staff as "stage productions," as each bears the distinctive stylings of Joyce Conwy Evans, an English set designer who, before finishing her work, had never set foot in the inn, or in America for that matter. Each room features interesting angles, yards of inventively draped fabrics, and bold wall coverings.

Room 7 (low $400 range), one of the front-facing corner rooms on the second floor, has a balcony with comfortable seating. Inside, a king-sized bed sits under a papered coffered ceiling.

One of the most unusual accommodations is room 4 (mid $300 range), where paisleys, florals, and plaids are tastefully and beautifully mixed. Framed tarot cards adorn every wall, and there's also a cozy window seat.

On the third floor, suite 9 (mid $500 range) is one of our favorites. It features a sitting room with a beautiful couch set within a stunning alcove, a garden-view balcony, and a large bathroom with a spa tub for one placed beneath a window. The bed is found in a loft under the eaves. There's also a nice dressing area with a built-in couch.

The smallest and least expensive quarters, room 2 (mid $200 range) is a romantic hideaway with a wonderful window seat and a magnificent vaulted ceiling, two chairs, and a queen-sized bed. The bathroom is equipped with a shower.

The growing popularity of the inn resulted in a 1997 expansion of the restaurant and the creation of two new suites, one of which is equipped with a fireplace, a spacious bathroom, and a balcony.

L'AUBERGE PROVENÇALE

Route 340
P.O. Box 119
White Post, VA 22663
Telephone: (540) 837-1375; toll-free: (800) 638-1702

Eleven rooms, each with private bath; six with fireplaces.
Complimentary full breakfast served at tables for two in
the inn's restaurant. Handicapped access. Smoking is not
permitted. Expensive to deluxe.

Getting There
From Washington, D.C., on Interstate 66 west, take exit
23 to Highway 17 north. Follow for nine miles to
Highway 50. Turn left (west) and continue to Highway
340. Turn south on Route 340 and continue for one mile
to inn on the right.

L'AUBERGE PROVENÇALE ❧ White Post

We're always a bit suspicious of inns that bill themselves as offering the best in cuisine and overnight accommodations. All too often we find that either the bedrooms are dowdy and the meals great, or the bedrooms are enticing but the food is poor. L'Auberge Provençale manages this challenging double billing masterfully.

This quaint property, a two-hundred-year-old stone farmhouse and a newer wing of country French–style quarters, derives much of its personality from its delightful owners, Celeste Borel and her husband, Alain, a fourth-generation master chef who serves up memorable multicourse dinners and breakfasts. Fixed-price dinners are offered to guests and passersby for around $60 per person.

ROOMS FOR ROMANCE

We spent a most memorable night savoring La Suite Romantique (mid $200 range), the end unit in the newer Les Chambres wing. Guests enter the two-room suite through a French door. The upper level is a sitting room with a dark wood floor, a French tiled fireplace, two sumptuous overstuffed chairs, and a small table. The bedroom, which sits behind a railing a couple of steps down, holds a king-sized alcove bed, a writing desk, and an armoire. A large Palladian window overlooks a bucolic country scene. The sexy bathroom has an Italian tiled floor, sponge-painted walls, and a big spa tub for two complete with candles.

Next door, room 10 (high $100 range) boasts a vibrant color scheme, a Shaker-style, pencil-post, queen-sized bed, and a Spanish tiled fireplace. The bathroom has a tub-and-shower combination with Mexican tiles.

In the main house, room 6 (mid $100 range) is a Colonial-style upstairs room with wide pine plank floors. There's a fireplace, a king-sized draped bed, and two wing chairs. The bathroom has a tub-and-shower combination.

The most romantic room in the main house is the Manor House Suite (around $200), which features a large private deck with outdoor furniture, a separate sitting room, and a bedroom furnished with a king-sized bed. The bathroom offers a spa tub for two and a shower stall.

THE INN AT VAUCLUSE SPRING

140 Vaucluse Spring Lane
Stephens City, VA 22655
Telephone: (540) 869-0200

Twelve rooms, each with private bath and at least one fireplace;
two with tubs for two. Complimentary full breakfast served at
tables for two; continental breakfast can be delivered to your
room. Dinner available for guests on Saturday nights. Swimming
pool and restaurant. Limited handicapped access. Smoking is not
permitted. Two-night minimum stay required during weekends
and holiday periods. Moderate to deluxe.

Getting There
From Washington, D.C., on Interstate 66 west, exit right onto
Interstate 81 north. Take exit 302 to Route 627 west toward
Middletown. Continue to the end of Route 627 and turn right on
Highway 11 north. Follow for two miles and turn left on Vaucluse
Spring Lane (Route 638). Inn is three-quarters of a mile on the left.

THE INN AT VAUCLUSE
SPRING ✧ Stephens City

For the late Virginia painter John Chumley, Vaucluse Spring was an artist's sanctuary, a quiet country haven where he raised a family and created many of his most famous works. These days, the famed artist's eclectic Stephens City compound is inspiring travelers in the fine art of romance.

Located just a few miles from the intersection of Interstates 81 and 66, the Inn at Vaucluse Spring is one of the most ambitious and pleasing inns we visited in the Mid-Atlantic states.

The sprawling property comprises not only three buildings that Chumley moved here but the old Strother Jones estate, whose centerpiece, a 1785 brick manor house, was rescued from decay and refurbished in grand style in 1997.

ROOMS FOR ROMANCE

The varied accommodations are spread among the manor house, the Chumley homestead, the Mill House Studio, and the Gallery Guest House, each of which offers a different guest experience.

We'll start our tour at the homeplace, which houses the comfortable public rooms and four guest rooms. In the Chumley Suite (mid $100 range), you'll enjoy the sitting room and the two-sided fireplace, which is visible from the bedroom and the bathroom. A view of Vaucluse Spring is also offered from this room.

A few steps away is the charming two-level Gallery Guest House (upper $100 range) that overlooks the swimming pool. On the first level is an attractive sitting room with a couch and pine floors. The upstairs bedroom with its dormer windows has a king-sized bed that faces a gas fireplace. The romantic bathroom holds an oval spa tub into which you might squeeze two.

Our personal favorite is the Mill House Studio (low to mid $200 range), where Chumley plied his craft. The studio hugs the edge of lovely Vaucluse Spring, whose constant outflow helps to set a soothing romantic mood. On the lower level of the studio is a couch and gas fireplace. A huge multipaned window frames the spring. There's even an easel with art supplies in case you're inspired to paint. The upstairs bedroom contains a king-sized brass bed, and the bathroom has an oval spa tub and a separate shower.

In the manor house, the most expensive accommodation (around $200) is the Jones Room, a corner hideaway with large windows, two overstuffed chairs, a gas fireplace, a queen-sized four-poster bed, and a pleasing tree and mountain view. The bathroom has its own fireplace as well as an oval spa tub.

We preferred the second-floor rooms to the three nice but somewhat earthy winter kitchen level (basement) rooms, with small windows set high in the rock walls.

Maryland

If your getaway takes you to the Oxford area, bring your bicycles on the three-hundred-year-old Oxford-Bellevue ferry—America's oldest—across the Tred Avon River and pedal around St. Michaels. The Chesapeake Bay Maritime Museum there is worth a visit.

An hour's drive from Washington, D.C., brings you to Frederick, whose charming thirty-three-block-long downtown district is worth exploring. There are three covered bridges in Frederick County.

In Snow Hill you can rent a canoe at the Pocomoke River Canoe Company or hop aboard Tillie the Tug, an open tour tug boat that plies the Pocomoke to Shad Landing and back.

Civil War buffs will want to visit Antietam, one of the best-preserved battlefields and also one of the least visited.

Tables for Two
The dining room of the Atlantic Hotel on North Main Street in Berlin is an elegant choice if you're spending the night at River House Inn (see listing in this section).

The late writer James Michener once proclaimed the crab cakes of the Robert Morris Inn (see listing in this section) the best on Maryland's Eastern Shore. In nearby St. Michaels, try the eponymous 208 Talbot.

Antrim 1844 (see listing in this section) is known not only for its romantic accommodations but for its fine multicourse dinners.

RIVER HOUSE INN

201 E. Market Street

Snow Hill, MD 21863

Telephone: (410) 632-2722

Eight rooms, each with private bath; six with fireplaces;
three with tubs for two. Complimentary full breakfast
served at tables for two. Handicapped access. Smoking is
not permitted. Two-night minimum stay required during
weekends and holiday periods. Moderate to expensive.

Getting There

From Highway 50 east, take Highway 13 bypass south.
Continue on Highway 13 for two and a half miles to
Route 12. Drive sixteen miles to Snow Hill and go over
the bridge to the light. Turn left on Market Street, then
left on Green Street to driveway of the inn on the right.

RIVER HOUSE INN ✍ Snow Hill

One of the most prominent residential landmarks in the picturesque Eastern Shore village of Snow Hill, River House Inn is an exquisite antique Victorian that dates back to the mid-1800s.

The grand residence is itself a sight to behold, but there's much more that's not apparent from the street. The rambling property also includes hidden romantic backyard hideaways and a wonderful rear lawn that sweeps down to the Pocomoke River. Watercraft may be rented nearby.

ROOMS FOR ROMANCE

Our highest recommendations go to the two honeymoon quality Riverview Hideaways (upper $100 range) found in a newer building overlooking the river. Colonial, the lower

level room, holds a fishnet canopied queen-sized bed, a gas fireplace, a corner spa tub for two, and a twenty-eight-foot private deck with wicker furniture overlooking the lawn, trees, and river. The bathroom has a tub-and-shower combination.

Upstairs is the Garden Room with a canopied iron bed and a layout and deck similar to that of Colonial. Each unit also has a microwave oven, a small refrigerator, a videocassette player, a television, and a coffeemaker.

Another option is the freestanding River Cottage (mid $100 range), a hundred-year-old converted carriage barn. This romantic gem has a king-sized bed facing a large window, a day bed for relaxing, and a screened porch with wicker furniture. The bathroom has a spa tub-and-shower combination.

If your choice is the stately main house, we're confining our recommendations to the East and West Rooms (low $100 range), the two front-facing rooms on the inn's second floor.

COMBSBERRY 1730

4837 Evergreen Road
Oxford, MD 21654
Telephone: (410) 226-5353

Six rooms, each with private bath; three with fireplaces.
Handicapped access. Smoking is not permitted. Deluxe.

Getting There
From Highway 301, take Highway 50 east to Route 322
south. Then take Route 333 south. Continue for about
seven miles and turn left on Evergreen Road. Take the
second left at brick entranceway.

COMBSBERRY 1730 ❧ Oxford

Readers of the *Weekends for Two* series know that in each edition we discover one or two hideaways that are so special we'd prefer to keep them to ourselves. In the Mid-Atlantic states, Combsberry is the secret we only somewhat reluctantly share with our readers.

Set very privately off the main highway at the end of a long private lane—Oxford village is a few minutes away by car—this magnificently restored 1730s-era home enjoys one of Maryland's most idyllic and romantic settings.

The inn sits among mature trees at the head of a scenic cove of Island Creek, which is a tidal flow of the north shore of the Choptank River. The water views are a feast for the eyes, and there's even a boat dock that guests may use.

ROOMS FOR ROMANCE

There are only four choices, and each is of honeymoon quality. Our personal favorite is the Magnolia Suite (around $400), which comprises half of the home's second floor. You are treated to a lovely view of the water as well as your own fireplace from the king-sized pencil-post bed. There's a separate dressing room through which you access a private deck.

The beautiful white tiled bath has a shower stall and a spa tub (maybe for two) set under a curved water-view window.

Next door is the Waterford Room (around $300), furnished with a queen-sized pencil-post bed, a fireplace, and deep rose wallpaper. There are water views from both the bedroom and the bathroom.

Access to the spacious Victoria Garden Room (around $300) is via a private outside entry from the garden or from inside the inn. This dormered room, which features a white, blue, and floral motif, is set beneath the eaves and has a queen-sized iron bed and two wicker chairs. The bath has a tub-and-shower combination.

Oxford Cottage (mid $300 range) is a romantic self-contained hideaway with a living room equipped with a love seat and a working fireplace; a tiny kitchen with a stove, a microwave, and a dishwasher; and a second-floor bedroom with three dormer windows. A small private brick patio overlooks the water.

Two nice guest rooms in the estate's carriage house are separated by a common area containing a living room with a fireplace, a dining room, and a kitchen.

ROBERT MORRIS INN

314 N. Morris Street (P.O. Box 70)
Oxford, MD 21654
Telephone: (410) 226-5111

Thirty-five rooms, each with private bath; three with
decorative fireplaces; two with tubs for two. Restaurant.
Handicapped access. Smoking is not permitted. Two-
night minimum stay required during weekends. Winter
operation varies from December through March.
Moderate to deluxe.

Getting There
From Highway 301, take Highway 50 east. Turn right on
Easton Parkway (Route 322) south. Turn right on Route
333 south and continue for ten miles to the inn.

ROBERT MORRIS INN ✍ Oxford

A night in historic simplicity or a night in romantic luxury? That's the biggest decision facing visitors to the Robert Morris Inn, a relaxed waterside hostelry offering a range of comfortable overnight accommodations that spans the ages of America.

The earliest part of the inn was built as a home during the early 1700s by ship carpenters, who employed wooden pegged paneling, ships' nails, and ballast for fireplaces. Among the first owners was Robert Morris, an English trading company executive whose son, Robert, Jr., signed the Declaration of Independence, the Articles of Confederation, and the Constitution.

The inn's intriguing restaurant is divided into three connected sections. Guests may choose either the formal dining room with its large murals made from antique wallpaper samples; the taproom, which is warmed by a fireplace; or the tavern, which boasts brick arches and a slate floor.

ROOMS FOR ROMANCE
The current proprietors have expanded overnight options through the acquisition of some nearby properties, including a summer house with lavish river-view suites.

If you elect to take a step back in time, try the circa 1710 part of the inn, where guest rooms are casually decorated and offer private baths. Room 15 (upper $100 range), a top choice, has a romantic poster bed with a three-step stool.

The Sandaway Lodge, located a half block from the inn, is a century-old summer house situated along two acres of private beach that are accessible to all guests. The most romantic rooms here are the River Rooms (mid $200 range), which overlook the Tred Avon River. Most of the Sandaway rooms offer sumptuous clawfoot tubs, screened porches, and pine paneling.

The Treehouse Room (around $200) is served by its own stairway, and room 202 (around $200) is equipped with a corner balcony.

There's also a freestanding cottage almost entirely surrounded by water. However, the bathroom is located in the Sandaway.

ASHBY 1663

27448 Ashby Drive (P.O. Box 45)
Easton, MD 21601
Telephone: (410) 822-4235

Fourteen rooms, each with private bath; eight with
fireplaces; four with tubs for two. Complimentary full
breakfast served at large communal table or tables for
two. Swimming pool. No handicapped access. Smoking
is not permitted. Two-night minimum stay required
during weekends. Deluxe.

Getting There
Take Highway 50 east across Bay Bridge to Easton. Turn
right at Airport Road, then right again at Goldsborough
Neck Road. Bear left at fork and continue to inn's
entrance and small sign on the left.

ASHBY 1663 ❧ Easton

When planning a romantic getaway, we typically first choose a favorite city or town and then select a suitable local place to spend the night. That's not the case with Ashby 1663, which is anything but an afterthought. It's a destination unto itself and one of Easton's greatest assets.

We hadn't intended to arrive so late, but the sun had already set when we reached the inn's white gates. The Italian villa–style mansion was still visible under the darkening sky, and every window was aglow. A family of deer nibbling at the vast lawn paid us little notice as we wound up the drive past the massive columned entry. The image of the imposing, well-lit

mansion lingered in our memory long after we had departed.

The Ashby estate is vast, occupying a heavenly peninsula in Maryland around which the Miles River flows. The property is dotted with oak and maple trees, and the swimming pool and tennis court are added bonuses.

Inside, you won't lack privacy in the public areas, as there are about as many sitting rooms as there are couples visiting. All are comfortably and lavishly decorated.

ROOMS FOR ROMANCE

Without a doubt, the sumptuous Robert Goldsborough Suite is one of the region's most romantic guest rooms. And at around $600 per night, it's also one of the most expensive. Although the suite's bedroom, with its king-sized canopied bed and fireplace, is impressive, the bathroom is the star attraction. The tiled, room-sized bath has its own fireplace, screened porch, dressing area, two-person shower, bidet, and spa tub for two.

The Charles Henry Room (high $300 range), our room for a night, occupies a comfortable corner on the mansion's third floor. Private view decks are accessible from both the bathroom and the bedroom. Furnishings include a queen-sized canopy bed, a desk, a wing chair, and an armoire with a television. The beautiful bathroom holds a deep spa tub for two set in a tiled and draped enclosure.

The Miles River Cabin is a new building that sits at water's edge. Among the luxurious rooms here are two second-floor hideaways with fireplaces, single spa tubs, and private decks overlooking the river.

The Todd Family Room, one of the inn's least expensive accommodations (around $200), is found in the George Goldsborough House. This room features a queen-sized four-poster bed and a sleeping loft.

GRAMERCY MANSION
BED AND BREAKFAST

1400 Greenspring Valley Road
Stevenson, MD 21153-0119
Telephone: (410) 486-2405

Ten rooms; five with private baths; three with fireplaces;
two with tubs for two. Complimentary full breakfast
served at tables for two. Swimming pool. No handicapped access. Smoking is not permitted. Moderate to
expensive.

Getting There
From downtown Baltimore, take Interstate 83 north to
Interstate 695 west to Pikesville/Towson. Take exit 22,
Greenspring Avenue. Drive north to first light at
Greenspring Valley Road. Turn left and continue to first
driveway on right.

GRAMERCY MANSION
BED AND BREAKFAST ✍ Stevenson

Unlike most couples who are given things like place settings and textiles as wedding presents, Eliza Cassatt and her husband received this house. The daughter of Pennsylvania Railroad baron Alexander Cassatt and the niece of the impressionist painter Mary Cassatt, Eliza was gifted this grand Tudor-style mansion upon her wedding at the turn of the century.

It was later owned by descendants of Benjamin Franklin, and during the 1950s it served as home for the Koinonia Foundation, a predecessor of the Peace Corps.

Located in an upscale community in Green Spring Valley, Gramercy Mansion is a quiet and convenient retreat offering a large swimming pool, tennis courts, and walking trails. Strolling the wooded grounds of the estate, it's hard to believe that bustling Baltimore is only twenty minutes away.

ROOMS FOR ROMANCE

Our favorite is the Blue Garden Suite (mid $200 range), an eclectically furnished retreat that has a nicely windowed step-down sitting room with a couch and chairs overlooking the inn's garden and swimming pool. The bedroom has an attractively draped ceiling and a king-sized bed, and the tiled bathroom has a deep spa tub for two.

The handsome Hunt Room (around $200) is done in hunter green and dark woods, and it features a king-sized four-poster bed and a marble bathroom with a spa tub for two.

There's a fireplace and a single spa tub in the Ambassador's Room (around $200). Another good choice and a romantic bargain is Aphrodite's Retreat (mid $100 range), a lacy room on the third floor with a dormered sitting area overlooking the swimming pool. The room has a full-sized bed and a chaise longue, and the tiny bathroom has a shower stall with a full body spray.

We do not recommend the back-hall rooms with single beds and shared hall bath.

ANTRIM 1844

30 Trevanion Road

Taneytown, MD 21787

Telephone: (410) 756-6812; toll-free: (800) 858-1844

Twenty-one rooms, each with private bath; ten with
fireplaces; seven with tubs for two. Complimentary full
breakfast served at tables for two and in your room.
Swimming pool and restaurant. No handicapped access.
Smoking is not allowed except in the pub. Two-night
minimum stay required during weekends and holiday
periods. Deluxe.

Getting There

From Interstate 695, take exit 19 (Highway 795 north) to
Highway 140 west to Taneytown, which is ten miles west
of Westminster. Turn left on Trevanion Road and drive
one hundred fifty feet to brick pillar entry on right. The
inn is 45 miles from Baltimore.

ANTRIM 1844   ✍   Taneytown

There's only one drawback to a visit to Antrim 1844. The inn's entrancing combination of wonderful food, swimming pool, tennis court, and ultra-romantic accommodations just might make you forget about all your other commitments. A visit to this all-in-one romantic retreat should come with a warning that Antrim 1844 may be hazardous to your sensibilities.

Formerly a thriving plantation, Antrim 1844 consists of an impressive Federal-style mansion and a number of exquisitely renovated outbuildings spread over twenty-four nicely maintained acres of lawn, century-old hedgerows, and pines.

Food is an integral part of a visit to Antrim 1844. Your day starts with fresh muffins, coffee, and a newspaper delivered to your door. A full breakfast is served a little later in the main

house. Dinners, which are popular among area residents as well as inn guests, are typically five courses from a menu that changes daily. The fixed-price dinner is offered for about $60 per person.

ROOMS FOR ROMANCE

Our favorite accommodations are located in the wonderfully refurbished outbuildings. The Ice House (mid $200 range), for example, is an unusually enchanting cottage with a stone foundation and two Dutch doors. The large romantic bathroom has a fireplace and a spa tub for two framed in wood and placed under a Palladian window.

The Barn, a remote cottage at the lower edge of the property, holds the Carriage and Sleigh Rooms (mid $200 range). Both have decks overlooking a stream. The Sleigh Room has a queen-sized canopy bed, a marble fireplace, and a bathroom with a romantic steam shower.

A spa tub for two and a two-person steam shower are among the attractions of the Taney Suite (around $300), located on the top floor of the Smith House, an antique brick farmhouse that was moved to the Antrim property.

We spent a night in the Boucher Suite (mid $200 range) in the main house, where a spacious and multiwindowed bedroom holds a king-sized bed whose canopy pattern matches the wallpaper. There's also a fireplace and an antique couch. The huge bathroom holds a bidet, two vanities, and a step-up marble-framed spa tub for two. Keep in mind that the shower is located in a small bathroom that's separate from the suite.

Six new rooms with romantic features such as spa tubs for two were created in a 1998 renovation of the inn's carriage house.

At the time of our visit, some of the main house rooms showed signs of peeling wallpaper, chipped paint, and stained upholstery, suggesting the need for a touch up here and there.

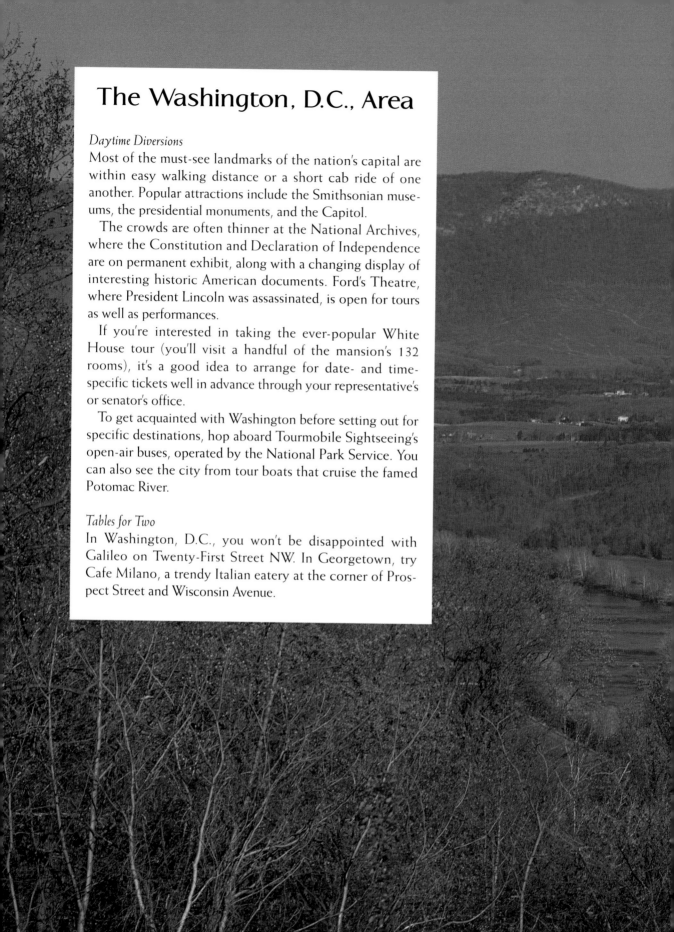

The Washington, D.C., Area

Daytime Diversions
Most of the must-see landmarks of the nation's capital are within easy walking distance or a short cab ride of one another. Popular attractions include the Smithsonian museums, the presidential monuments, and the Capitol.

The crowds are often thinner at the National Archives, where the Constitution and Declaration of Independence are on permanent exhibit, along with a changing display of interesting historic American documents. Ford's Theatre, where President Lincoln was assassinated, is open for tours as well as performances.

If you're interested in taking the ever-popular White House tour (you'll visit a handful of the mansion's 132 rooms), it's a good idea to arrange for date- and time-specific tickets well in advance through your representative's or senator's office.

To get acquainted with Washington before setting out for specific destinations, hop aboard Tourmobile Sightseeing's open-air buses, operated by the National Park Service. You can also see the city from tour boats that cruise the famed Potomac River.

Tables for Two
In Washington, D.C., you won't be disappointed with Galileo on Twenty-First Street NW. In Georgetown, try Cafe Milano, a trendy Italian eatery at the corner of Prospect Street and Wisconsin Avenue.

FOUR SEASONS HOTEL

2800 Pennsylvania Avenue NW
Washington, D.C. 20007
Telephone: (202) 342-0444

Two hundred fifty-six rooms and suites, each with private
bath; several with tubs for two. Swimming pool and
restaurant. Handicapped access. Smoking is allowed.
Deluxe.

Getting There
Heading into Washington, D.C., from Interstate 66 east,
take exit Rosslyn/Key Bridge. Continue and at third light
take a left on North Lynn Street. Cross Key Bridge in the
right lane and at the end of the bridge turn right on M
Street. Follow M Street nine blocks. After Twenty-ninth
Street, the hotel is on the right.

FOUR SEASONS HOTEL ❧ District of Columbia

There's nothing like spending a day exploring romantic Georgetown, except maybe spending an evening exploring Georgetown and a night at the ultraromantic Four Seasons Hotel.

Located on Pennsylvania Avenue at the entrance to this tony community, the Four Seasons overlooks the famous C&O Canal, which George Washington commissioned, and is conveniently close to the antique shops, boutiques, and restaurants of Georgetown. The Shops at Georgetown Park center is a short walk away.

The Four Seasons' contemporary red brick facade won't necessarily take your breath away; it's the pleasures inside that have made this one of D.C.'s most coveted places to stay. The public areas and restaurants are warm and refined, and the fitness center is one of the nicest and best equipped we've seen, offering a lap pool, an oversized whirlpool, hydrotherapy services, aerobic fitness machines, and steam and sauna rooms. The hotel's staff also make it a point to know your name.

ROOMS FOR ROMANCE

The hotel underwent an expansion in 1998 that boosted its size to two hundred fifty-six rooms. Accommodations here are tastefully appointed with plush, comfortable chairs, soft lighting, plants, and terry bathrobes. Rates begin in the high $300 range for a "moderate" room with a queen-sized bed. "Superior" status (around $400) includes a king-sized bed, while a "deluxe" room (low $400 range) offers a king-sized bed in more spacious surroundings.

A plush one-bedroom Executive or Plaza suite (low $700 range) includes an elegantly furnished sitting area and a separate bedroom, along with two bathrooms. Suites also come with videocassette players and compact disc players.

Rates quoted above are for weekdays. Be sure to inquire about more reasonable weekend rates, which start below $300 per night.

JEFFERSON HOTEL
Sixteenth & M Streets NW
Washington, D.C. 20036-3295
Telephone: (202) 347-2200; toll-free: (800) 368-5966

One hundred rooms, each with private bath; two with
fireplaces; two with tubs for two. Restaurant. Handicapped access. Smoking is allowed. Moderate to deluxe.

Getting There
North of Washington, D.C., take Interstate 495 to exit
33, Connecticut Avenue. Continue south toward the city
until you reach Dupont Circle. Take a left on Massachu-
setts Avenue NW. Take a right on Sixteenth Street. The
hotel is on the right.

JEFFERSON HOTEL ☙ District of Columbia

During the work week, the noble Jefferson bustles with businesspeople and government types who appreciate the hotel's central D.C. location and its modern conveniences, like in-room two-line speaker phones and fax machines. During the weekends, the rooms here are occupied by folks who have a less hectic agenda, and who have time to savor the canopy beds, terry robes, and each other.

Among the many American city hotels whose romantic potential we've sampled, the Jefferson is a standout. In terms of location, size, comfort, and service, it's one of the best.

Those looking for a strategic base from which to visit the landmarks of the nation's capital will be well served by the Jefferson. From here, it's a four-block walk to the White House. The memorials, the Smithsonian Museums, and the National Archives are within a healthy walk or a short cab ride away, and the shops of Connecticut Avenue are two blocks from the hotel.

The Jefferson started out in the 1920s as an upscale society residence, and it hosted military personnel during World War II. A complete renovation in the late 1980s restored the property's original luster.

ROOMS FOR ROMANCE

One of the attractions of the Jefferson is the varied guest room decor. Your room might be decorated in French provincial furniture, while the couple next door are enjoying an English-inspired experience.

Suite 803 (low to high $200 range), our hideaway for a night, is a luxurious corner suite with lots of windows, antique lithographs, and views of neighboring buildings. The large sitting room holds a couch, a large table, and an armoire concealing a television, videocassette player, and compact disc player. In the bedroom is a king-sized bed, a chair with ottoman, a desk, and another armoire with a television and a videocassette player. The modern marbled bathroom has brass fixtures and a tub-and-shower combination.

Although the hotel's rooms are all comfortable, tasteful, and well equipped, the most inspired accommodations are the suites, which we recommend for a memorable romantic getaway. Ask about special packages when you make a reservation.

THE BAILIWICK INN

4023 Chain Bridge Road
Fairfax, VA 22030
Telephone: (703) 691-2266; toll-free: (800) 366-7666

Fourteen rooms, each with private bath; four with woodburning fireplaces; two with tubs for two. Complimentary full breakfast served in the inn's restaurant. Smoking is not permitted. No minimum-night stay required. Moderate to deluxe.

Getting There

From Interstate 66, take exit 60 Fairfax (Route 123) south. Proceed through four traffic lights, then turn left on Sager Avenue and follow to inn at the corner of Route 123 and Sager Avenue.

THE BAILIWICK INN ❧ Fairfax, Virginia

Visitors to Washington, D.C., who choose the nearby Bailiwick Inn as their base not only have an opportunity to visit history but to romance it. The Bailiwick, whose address is the nation's oldest toll road, sits across the street from the courthouse in which the will of George Washington was filed. A battle fought across the inn's front lawn claimed the first Confederate casualty of the Civil War.

Known for generations as the "house across from the courthouse," the inn draws its name from the earliest meaning of the word *bailiwick*: the area around the court.

This handsome, early 1800s Federal-style landmark has weathered nearly two centuries quite gracefully, thanks to an artful renovation that preserved the building's historic significance while providing contemporary travelers with all the comforts of home, and then some. Although it's fifteen miles from Washington, D.C., the inn enjoys a convenient location halfway between Dulles Airport and the nation's capital. Restaurants and interesting shops are steps away.

ROOMS FOR ROMANCE

Antonia Ford, a beautiful Confederate spy, is the namesake for the inn's bridal suite (around $300), a luscious top-floor hideaway that has a Chippendale-furnished sitting room, a bedroom with a king-sized four-poster bed, dormer windows, and a bathroom equipped with a spa tub for two set in tile below a dormer.

A spa tub for two is also found in the Nellie Custis Room (around $200), which overlooks the nearby courthouse from the inn's third floor.

The George Mason Room (around $200) is a cozy second-floor corner room where a canopied queen-sized bed sits before a handsome fireplace flanked by built-in bookshelves. This room also has a chaise longue and a wing chair.

Red and gold is the rich theme for the Thomas Jefferson Room (around $200), which has a fireplace, large windows, and a canopied queen-sized bed draped in crimson damask.

Be aware that the James Madison Room's private bathroom is accessed off the hallway.

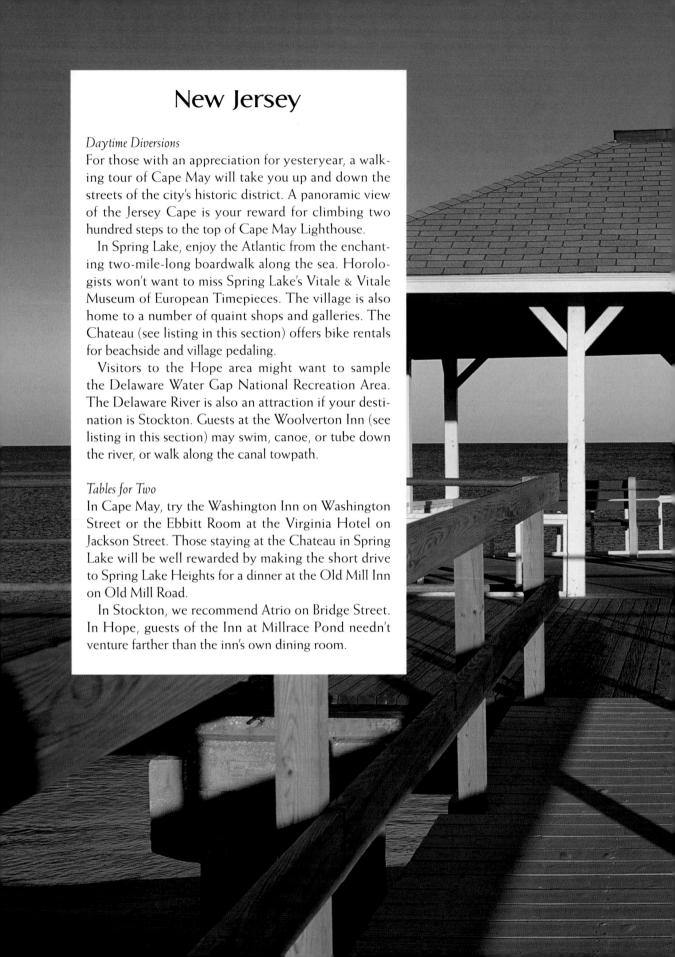

New Jersey

Daytime Diversions

For those with an appreciation for yesteryear, a walking tour of Cape May will take you up and down the streets of the city's historic district. A panoramic view of the Jersey Cape is your reward for climbing two hundred steps to the top of Cape May Lighthouse.

In Spring Lake, enjoy the Atlantic from the enchanting two-mile-long boardwalk along the sea. Horologists won't want to miss Spring Lake's Vitale & Vitale Museum of European Timepieces. The village is also home to a number of quaint shops and galleries. The Chateau (see listing in this section) offers bike rentals for beachside and village pedaling.

Visitors to the Hope area might want to sample the Delaware Water Gap National Recreation Area. The Delaware River is also an attraction if your destination is Stockton. Guests at the Woolverton Inn (see listing in this section) may swim, canoe, or tube down the river, or walk along the canal towpath.

Tables for Two

In Cape May, try the Washington Inn on Washington Street or the Ebbitt Room at the Virginia Hotel on Jackson Street. Those staying at the Chateau in Spring Lake will be well rewarded by making the short drive to Spring Lake Heights for a dinner at the Old Mill Inn on Old Mill Road.

In Stockton, we recommend Atrio on Bridge Street. In Hope, guests of the Inn at Millrace Pond needn't venture farther than the inn's own dining room.

ANGEL OF THE SEA BED AND BREAKFAST

5 Trenton Avenue

Cape May, NJ 08204

Telephone toll-free: (800) 848-3369

Twenty-seven rooms and suites, each with private bath.
Complimentary full breakfast served at communal tables.
Complimentary afternoon tea and sweets and evening wine and
cheese. Off-street parking. Free use of bikes and beach equipment.
Handicapped access. Smoking is allowed on verandas. Two- and
three-night minimum stay required during weekends, depending
on season. Expensive to deluxe for recommended rooms.

Getting There

From Garden State Parkway, take exit O and follow the signs into
Cape May. This becomes Lafayette Street. Turn left on Sidney
Street, left on Washington Street, and right at the traffic island.
Follow Pittsburgh Avenue to Beach Drive and turn right. Turn
right again at the next street. The inn is on the right.

ANGEL OF THE SEA
BED AND BREAKFAST ✍ Cape May

The pair of magnificent structures that comprise Angel of the Sea Bed and Breakfast appear as though they were made for this spot overlooking the Atlantic, but history tells a different story. The two buildings were built as a single home in 1850 by William Weightman, the Philadelphia chemist who perfected the use of quinine for medicinal use. He erected the massive residence a few blocks to the west, but later he decided to move closer to the beach. The home was literally cut in two and rolled on logs to another location, and in 1962 the structures were moved yet again to their present site a half block from the ocean. Today, the two impressively refurbished halves are connected by a walkway.

The inn, which drips with gingerbread and boasts fancy turrets, dormers, and towers, is one of the most prominent buildings along Cape May's coast. The beach is just a few steps away.

ROOMS FOR ROMANCE

Rooms here, which feature attractive wallpaper and antique reproduction furnishings, are categorized as standard, deluxe, deluxe queen, premier, premier deluxe, and angel suite. We looked at a number of rooms and found the standard and deluxe rooms a bit small and cramped, especially for a couple wanting to enjoy a memorable romantic getaway.

Room 6, a deluxe queen bedroom, is a wonderful corner hideaway with a semi-private veranda, lots of windows, and an ocean view. The furniture is wicker and the room is nicely wallpapered.

Room 9, in the premiere category, holds a queen-sized four-poster bed and has a sitting area with two wing chairs. The room faces the front and side and offers an ocean view and access to a veranda. The tiny bath has a shower stall. The handsome ceiling in this and the other guest rooms is made of dark wainscoting. There are approximately twenty miles of this material placed tongue-and-groove style throughout the inn.

It takes a complex rate card to follow the tariffs, which fluctuate wildly with the change of seasons. The least expensive time to visit is the winter and fall, when nightly rates range from the low $100 range for a deluxe room to the mid $200 range for a suite. In July and August, plan on spending at least $50 to $70 more per night.

THE MAINSTAY INN

635 Columbia Avenue
Cape May, NJ 08204
Telephone: (609) 884-8690

Sixteen rooms, each with private bath; four with fireplaces;
four with tubs for two. Complimentary full or continental
(depending on the season) breakfast served at communal
table or in your room. Some off-street parking. Handicapped access. Smoking is not permitted. Two- to three-
night minimum stay required during weekends; three-
to four-night minimum during holiday periods. Expensive
to deluxe.

Getting There
From Garden State Parkway, take exit O and follow the
signs into Cape May. This becomes Lafayette Street. Turn
left at Madison, then right on Columbia. Continue for
three blocks to inn on the right.

THE MAINSTAY INN   Cape May

During our Mid-Atlantic travels, which took us from Lake Placid, New York, to Williams-burg, Virginia, nowhere did we find an inn whose architectural beauty outshined the Mainstay Inn. Even in a city renowned for its grand Victorian buildings, this Atlantic Coast jewel is a traffic stopper, not to mention one of the most popular romantic getaway destinations in the region.

The Mainstay was built in the latter half of the nineteenth century as an opulent gentlemen's entertainment club, and the pair of wealthy gamblers who built it spared no expense. The many original and preserved features—fourteen-foot ceilings, a cupola, a broad veranda, refined walnut furniture, and fancy chandeliers—are evidence of the extravagance heaped upon this Italianate villa.

The architect responsible for the former men's club also designed the handsome adjacent home, which is part of the inn. The most recent addition is the Officers' Quarters across the street, which housed military families during World War I and has since been refurbished as

a luxurious romantic hideaway. The Mainstay property is located two blocks from Cape May's downtown and three blocks from the beach.

ROOMS FOR ROMANCE
Among the six rooms in the main building is the Henry Clay Room (mid $100 range), a front-facing second-floor beauty that's equipped with its original ornately carved, high Renaissance–style, queen-sized bed and armoire. You step up to a bathroom with eight-foot-high windows and a tub-and-shower combination. The main house is not air conditioned.

One of the most popular rooms in the next-door cottage is the Bret Harte Room (upper $100 range), with its handsome antique, high-styled, walnut queen-sized bed, matching dresser, and private veranda. The small but tasteful marbled bathroom has a glass-enclosed tub-and-shower combination.

As we awoke in Suite C (low $200 range), one of four accommodations in the Officers' Quarters, the rising sun illuminated the pastel painted ladies along Columbia Avenue. This very large second-floor suite holds two bedrooms. In the rear-facing bedroom, a queen-sized four-poster bed sits under a high ceiling with a fan. Walls are nicely papered, and a television is placed in a door chest. In the living area is a gas fireplace with an oak mantel, a sitting area with a love seat and a rocker, an antique writing desk, a table and chairs, a china cabinet, and a wet bar with a small refrigerator, a small microwave, and a coffeemaker. French doors lead to a covered porch furnished with wooden rockers. The marble-floored bathroom holds a faux granite–topped sink and an oval spa tub for two under a stained-glass window. There's also a separate shower stall.

The Officers' Quarters are open year-round; the other buildings are closed January through mid-March.

THE CHATEAU

500 Warren Avenue
Spring Lake, NJ 07762
Telephone: (732) 974-2000

Thirty-eight rooms, each with private bath; eleven
with fireplaces; ten with tubs for two. Breakfast is not
included. Handicapped access. Smoking is allowed.
Two- to three-night minimum stay required during
weekends; two- to four-night minimum during holiday
periods. Expensive to deluxe for recommended rooms.

Getting There
Follow the Garden State Parkway to exit 98. Then take
Highway 138 east. Continue for two miles, then take
Route 35 south. Drive two miles to the second stoplight
(Warren Avenue, but not marked). Turn left and drive just
over one mile to the inn.

THE CHATEAU ✑ Spring Lake

Although it's not widely heralded as one of the Mid-Atlantic region's most romantic destinations, the quaint, seaside community of Spring Lake, located an hour or so from Philadelphia, Atlantic City, and New York, is a delightful place to spend a night or two. It's especially romantic if your home base is one of the Chateau's parlor rooms or suites.

This Victorian-style hotel occupies a scenic spot between two parks and overlooking picturesque Spring Lake. The neighborhood, perfect for romantic strolling, includes charming older residences and is close to the village's downtown and to the ocean. You can rent bicycles at the inn for a nominal fee; summer guests receive free beach passes.

ROOMS FOR ROMANCE

You shouldn't have any trouble making fond romantic memories in either a luxury parlor room (low $200 range) or luxury parlor suite (low to mid $200 range), which are our recommended accommodations. Rates during the winter, spring, and fall months are considerably less.

Room 43, a luxury parlor room carpeted in cranberry, is a spacious hideaway with a corner fireplace, a couch, and a king-sized bed placed to take advantage of the park view. The bathroom has a large sumptuous soaking tub. Room 28, another luxury parlor room, has a step-up bedroom, a balcony, and a park view. The small bathroom has an oval soaking tub into which two might fit.

Room 42 is a luxury suite with a private outdoor entrance. The suite has a park-view sitting room with a fireplace, a couch, and a television. The separate bedroom has a king-sized bed, and the bathroom contains a large teardrop-shaped soaking tub.

A balcony and a fireplace are two romantic features found behind the door of room 27, another wonderful luxury suite.

THE WOOLVERTON INN

6 Woolverton Road
Stockton, NJ 08559
Telephone: (609) 397-0802

Ten rooms, each with private bath; two with fireplaces; two with tubs for two. Complimentary full breakfast served at communal table or tables for two. A continental breakfast may be taken to your room. Handicapped access. Smoking is not permitted. Two-night minimum stay required during weekends and holiday periods. Moderate to expensive.

Getting There
Take Highway 202 west toward Pennsylvania. Just before the Delaware River, take Route 29 north into Stockton. Two-tenths of a mile past Bridge Street, turn right on Route 523. Continue and turn left on Woolverton Road. The inn is the second driveway on the right.

THE WOOLVERTON INN   ✍   Stockton

Had the builders of the manor house known today as the Woolverton Inn chosen a spot just a few hundred yards away on the other side of the Delaware River, we'd be including this romantic getaway destination among our featured spots in Pennsylvania's famed Bucks County. Although it carries a New Jersey address, the Woolverton Inn is

a great base from which to explore eastern Pennsylvania as well as New Jersey's scenic western regions.

This handsome inn, whose strong stone facade is softened by white shutters and sculpted verandas, is tucked discreetly just outside the village of Stockton among fruit trees and gardens. Four hundred acres of gently rolling farmland surround the inn. Croquet and horseshoes are among the simple pastimes available here, and the Delaware River and adjacent canal towpath are both easily accessible to guests.

ROOMS FOR ROMANCE

Originally the manor's master suite, Amelia's Partiere (high $100 range) is carpeted in hunter green, and an antique trunk sits at the foot of a king-sized four-poster bed with a lace canopy. A couch, a table, and two Windsor chairs comprise the sitting area. The bathroom has a tub-and-shower combination.

A contemporary bathroom with a step-up oval-shaped spa tub is the centerpiece for Letitia's Repose (high $100 range), a spacious suite that also has a beautiful, partially canopied king-sized bed and a fireplace.

On the third floor is Stockton's Quay (high $100 range), a large corner suite with an impressive bathroom appointed with Chinese slate. The bathroom is equipped with a spa tub for two and a separate shower, and the bedroom has a queen-sized bed with a twig headboard.

There are two rooms (mid $100 range) located in an adjacent carriage house. The decorating theme of one of these hideaways is captured in its name: Bodine's Farm. In the other room, Willets Garden, vines are painted on the walls. Both rooms have queen-sized beds.

For romantic getaways, we were not as impressed with the Primrose Room or Caroline's Room, both of which have detached bathrooms, or with Asher's Glen or Dorothy's Alcove.

THE INN AT MILLRACE POND

Route 519 (P.O. Box 359)
Hope, NJ 07844
Telephone: (908) 459-4884

Seventeen rooms, each with private bath; one with
fireplace. Complimentary continental breakfast served at
tables for two. Restaurant. Handicapped access. Smoking
is allowed. Two-night minimum stay required during
weekends and holiday periods. Moderate to expensive.

Getting There
From Route 80, take exit 12. Turn on Route 521 south
and continue one mile to the blinking red stop light.
Turn left on Route 519. The inn is two-tenths of a mile
on the left.

THE INN AT MILLRACE POND ❧ Hope

For nearly two centuries, this pleasing stone structure saw duty as a gristmill whose earliest customers included George Washington's troops. Today it's a romantic inn whose customers have included Barbra Streisand, Dustin Hoffman, and other well-known folks.

The origins of the Inn at Millrace Pond are evident as you enter the building. The remnants of the historic waterwheel are on permanent view below you, and, if you visit during the spring or summer, you might see a trickle of water still flowing through the old millrace channel.

On the bottom level of the inn is an enchanting Colonial-style tavern with a brick floor and a fireplace big enough to stand in. The inn's dining room also features Colonial decor and is open daily for dinner; in addition, you'll find a tennis court on-site. The innkeepers are happy to arrange tee times at a nearby golf course, and if it's a warm day, they may treat you to a ride in their vintage Cadillac touring car.

ROOMS FOR ROMANCE

The former gristmill contains the majority of guest rooms, and these feature reproductions of Shaker-style furniture as well as the building's original pine floors. The rooms on the top floor have dramatic beamed cathedral ceilings. Rates here are in the mid to upper $100 range.

A more formal style pervades the six bedrooms (around $100 to mid $100 range) found in the Millrace House, which originally was home to the resident miller. This building also has a parlor with a fireplace.

The wheelwright resided in the secluded Stone Cottage, which houses two suites (mid $100 range) coveted by traveling romantics and Hollywood notables. There's one unit upstairs and another on the main floor, and each has a private entrance.

Pennsylvania

Daytime Diversions

In Chadds Ford, paintings by the resident Wyeth family and other American artists hang in the Brandywine River Museum, a restored antique gristmill on the Brandywine River. A mile-long walking trail takes you from the museum to the old stone home of the community's namesake, ferryman John Chadds.

Guests of the Rittenhouse Hotel have Philadelphia at their feet. The city's Antique Row is nearby, and Independence Park is about a half-hour walk away.

In New Hope, Bucks County, you can take a lazy cruise along the Delaware Canal on a mule-drawn barge or hop aboard the New Hope & Ivyland Rail Road for a scenic nine-mile trip. The Bristol Riverside Theater in Bristol is Bucks County's premiere professional theater. The New Hope Winery is one of several Bucks County winemaking operations.

Winter visitors to State College may sample nearby Tussey Mountain ski resort. The golf course adjacent to Carnegie House becomes a cross-country skiing course during the winter months.

The Pocono Playhouse in Mountainhome is one of the nation's oldest summer theaters. Callie's Candy Kitchen and Pretzel Factory, with outlets in Mountainhome and Cresco, is a sweet lover's paradise.

Tables for Two

Our Bucks County innkeepers recommend the Frenchtown Inn in Frenchtown, New Jersey, and La Bonne Auberge and Odette's, both in New Hope.

In Philadelphia, Le Bec-Fin is a famous and formal French restaurant. Suzanna Foo offers gourmet Chinese cuisine. Both are on Walnut Street.

In State College, Le Papillon is within walking distance of Carnegie House. The Tavern is another favorite in this popular college town.

BRANDYWINE RIVER HOTEL

Route 1 and Route 100 (P.O. Box 1058)

Chadds Ford, PA 19317-1058

Telephone: (610) 388-1200

Forty rooms, each with private bath; several with fireplaces and tubs for two. Complimentary continental breakfast included. Handicapped access. Smoking is permitted in some rooms. No minimum night stay required. Expensive to deluxe.

Getting There

Take Highway 1 west from North Philadelphia. The hotel is located at the intersection of Highway 1 and Route 100 in Chadds Ford, about twenty-five minutes from the Philadelphia airport.

BRANDYWINE RIVER HOTEL ✍ Chadds Ford

For generations, the Brandywine Valley and the community of Chadds Ford have inspired the resident Wyeth family to artistic greatness. But even if you are not as artistically inclined as the talented Wyeth clan, the beauty of Chadds Ford should definitely inspire you in the area of romance, particularly if you're staying the night in a sumptuous suite at the Brandywine River Hotel.

The hotel is a contemporary brick building with attractive Colonial touches. Set on a gentle hillside overlooking Chadds Ford, it's a popular home base for business travelers during the work week, but on the weekends it's filled with folks more interested in exploring the Brandywine River Valley. Hagley Museum, Winterthur Museum, and a famous Civil War battlefield are all within a fifteen-minute drive of the hotel. The Philadelphia airport is about a half hour away.

ROOMS FOR ROMANCE

The standard rooms and Executive Suites are comfortable but not distinctively romantic. For a truly memorable getaway we recommend a suite with a fireplace and spa tub for two. The ten Fireside Suites (upper $100 range) have sitting areas with sofas, tables and chairs, woodburning fireplaces, refrigerators, separate showers, and spa tubs for two. Some tubs are bigger than others, so ask for one of the large ones, if available.

There are two larger Premium Suites (upper $100 range) that are also equipped with fireplaces and spa tubs for two.

Some rooms at the Brandywine River Hotel have pleasing pasture views. Others look out over the parking area toward the village.

At the time of our visit, the hotel offered a romantic rendezvous package (mid $300 range) that included two nights in a suite with spa and fireplace, a gift certificate for dinner at a local restaurant, and wine and roses on arrival. Other packages were also available.

THE RITTENHOUSE HOTEL

210 W. Rittenhouse Square
Philadelphia, PA 19103
Telephone: (215) 546-9000; toll-free: (800) 635-1042

Ninety-eight rooms, each with private bath; five with
tubs for two. Swimming pool and restaurant. Handicapped access. Smoking is allowed. Expensive to deluxe.

Getting There
From Interstate 95 south, take the Center City exit to
Interstate 676 west. Follow 676 west to the Ben Franklin
Parkway exit. Turn right on Ben Franklin Parkway and
right on Twenty-first Street. Follow Twenty-first Street to
Chestnut Street. Turn left on Chestnut and then right on
Nineteenth Street. Turn right on Walnut Street and a
quick left on W. Rittenhouse Square. The hotel driveway
is the next right.

THE RITTENHOUSE HOTEL   ✑   Philadelphia

Philadelphia's smallest luxury hotel is proof that wonderful things do come in small packages. Just ask Tom Hanks who stayed in the fashionable Rittenhouse during the filming of *Philadelphia*, or singers Luciano Pavarotti and Billy Joel, who have also signed the guest register here.

Ideally located for walking tours of Philadelphia, this tall, slender hotel enjoys a picturesque spot across the street from the lovely Rittenhouse Square in a lively residential neighborhood just a short stroll from the city's financial district.

In addition to offering just under one hundred stylish guest rooms, the hotel has two impressive restaurants, including the attractive TreeTops, whose tiered seating areas afford nice views of the square. The hotel's fully equipped spa has a skylit indoor pool, fitness equipment, a steam room, and a sauna.

ROOMS FOR ROMANCE
We can hardly imagine more romantic accommodations than suite 920, where we spent a crisp winter night. The opulent retreat goes for around $500 during the week but drops to the mid $300 range during weekends. Boasting a handsome Ralph Lauren motif, the suite includes a living room with a couch and desk, as well as an assortment of chairs and lamps. The bedroom holds a king-sized bed, two wing chairs, and a dressing table. Both the living room and bedroom have televisions. In the bathroom is a shower stall, an oval shaped soaking tub barely big enough for two, a telephone, and a small television. A number of other suites feature more feminine Laura Ashley appointments.

The hotel's Deluxe Rooms (around $200) are spacious and luxurious, offering king-sized beds and irregular angles that make for interesting and inviting spaces. Separate sitting areas are furnished with either two large chairs or love seats. The marble bathrooms, which are likewise large, include separate tubs and showers as well as televisions.

Couples traveling together might want to consider one of the Rittenhouse's condominium-style accommodations, with two bedrooms, a living and a dining room, and a full kitchen.

THE INN AT TWIN LINDEN

2092 Main Street

Churchtown, PA 17555 ·

Telephone: (717) 445-7619

Seven rooms, each with private bath; three with fireplaces; two with tubs for two. Complimentary full breakfast served at tables for two. Outdoor Jacuzzi. No handicapped access. Smoking is not permitted. Two-night minimum stay required during weekends and holiday periods. Closed January. Moderate to deluxe.

Getting There

From the Pennsylvania Turnpike (Interstate 76), take exit 22 to Route 10 south. Then take Route 23 west for four miles into Churchtown. The inn is on the left side of Route 23 (Main Street).

THE INN AT TWIN LINDEN ❧ Churchtown

From the street, the Inn at Twin Linden doesn't appear too much different from the clean, well-kept homes of the region's Mennonites and Amish. But don't come to this beguiling inn expecting to sample the simple and plain way of life that has made Lancaster County famous. Tempting its guests with treats like Godiva chocolates, spa tubs for two, and multi-course dinners, the Inn at Twin Linden is anything but ordinary.

Travelers wanting to explore Amish country will be well served by using this Greek Revival–style inn as a central base. Horse-drawn carriages pass in front of and behind the inn, nearby Amish farms may be toured, and quilt and country shops abound. That's if you can pull yourself away from your room.

The inn, which sits among two and a half acres of gardens, is located along Route 23 in the quiet community of Churchtown. Two mature linden trees, the inn's namesakes, preside over an outdoor hot tub from which the two of you can view Amish and Mennonite farms. Fixed-price dinners are offered during weekends.

ROOMS FOR ROMANCE

You can't do better than the Palladian Suite (low $200 range), which is accessed through a private entry off the back porch. The room affords a lovely view of the Welsh Mountains and local farms, and it has a television, videocassette player, and a compact disc player should you desire further entertainment. The tiled bathroom has a deep spa tub for two set in black tile, and there's also a shower stall. A pellet stove placed at the foot of the bed will warm your toes on those cold winter nights.

We were also impressed with the second-floor Linden Room (mid to upper $100 range), which has a queen-sized bed with a lacy canopy, a gas fireplace, and a spa tub that might fit two.

The handsome Polo Room (mid $100 range) has dark furnishings and a queen-sized bed with a fishnet canopy, while the Sarah Jenkins Room (mid $100 range) features a more feminine motif in blue and white hues.

CLEARVIEW FARM BED AND BREAKFAST

355 Clearview Road
Ephrata, PA 17522
Telephone: (717) 733-6333

Five rooms, each with private bath. Complimentary full breakfast
served at communal table. No handicapped access. Smoking is not
permitted. Two-night minimum stay required during weekends and
holiday periods. Moderate.

Getting There
From Lancaster, take Route 272 north to Highway 322 west. After
passing the restaurant on right, take the fifth road right (Clearview
Road) to the first property on the right. Clearview Farm is about
four miles from Route 272.

CLEARVIEW FARM
BED AND BREAKFAST   ➳   Ephrata

If you've ever drifted through Pennsylvania's Dutch country and imagined what it might be like to spend a weekend on one of the engaging farms that dot the countryside, daydream no more. Clearview Farm Bed and Breakfast combines a farm experience with luxury accommodations, making for a most memorable Lancaster County getaway.

The handsome three-story, red-shuttered limestone inn is set against a gentle slope overlooking a pond and farmland. Surrounded by a lush lawn, the manor shares the expansive property with various farm buildings.

Visitors to Clearview Farm should be aware that the inn enjoys a tranquil rural setting about five miles from the town of Ephrata, so don't expect walking access to shops and restaurants. This is a working farm, and guest activities here run more toward watching the resident swans and curling up with a good book and your partner.

ROOMS FOR ROMANCE

The striking centerpieces of the Royal Room are an intricately carved Victorian bed and a complementary carved étagère filled with knickknacks. There are two comfy antique chairs for relaxing, and the bathroom is equipped with a clawfoot tub and shower.

On the feminine side is the Princess Room, a nicely wallpapered hideaway with a queen-sized bed dripping in lace. The bathroom has a tub-and-shower combination.

High on the third floor are the Washington and Lincoln Rooms, two romantic chambers that boast exposed stone walls, the inn's original wide board floors, and hand-pegged rafters. The Washington Room also has a rustic stone wall, an elegant canopied queen-sized bed, and a nice bathroom with a shower. The Lincoln Room is furnished with a queen-sized pencil-post tester bed and two wing chairs.

Rates at Clearview Farm are in the low to mid $100 range.

THE MERCERSBURG INN

405 S. Main Street
Mercersburg, PA 17236
Telephone: (717) 328-5231

Fifteen rooms, each with private bath; three with
fireplaces; three with tubs for two. Complimentary
full breakfast served at tables for two. Restaurant.
No handicapped access. Smoking is not permitted.
Two-night minimum stay required on weekends
during peak periods. Moderate to expensive.

Getting There
South of Harrisburg on Interstate 81, take exit 3
to Route 16 west. Drive ten miles to Mercersburg.
The inn is on the left as you enter Mercersburg.

THE MERCERSBURG INN ❧ Mercersburg

For those of us who must go through life adhering to a budget, a visit to a showplace like the Mercersburg Inn is an eye-popping experience. Down to the most minute detail, this exquisitely crafted estate is an example of what unlimited wealth can create. And it's yours, if only for a night or two.

The original owners were the fabulously wealthy Harry and Ione Byron, who made their fortune in the tanning business. In creating their dream home, the Byrons insisted on the finest—a slate roof, Indiana limestone sills, copper spouts, and inlaid white oak flooring. The columns of the grand hall underwent an expensive and painstaking process in which dyed silk threads were pulled through wet plaster to create a marblelike finish.

ROOMS FOR ROMANCE

Today, the grand residence holds fifteen guest rooms. Adding bathrooms to all the rooms presented some retrofitting challenges, resulting in some unusually placed baths. Some are small and purely functional.

Among the nicest rooms is room 2 (around $200), which is at the top of the stairs and faces front. The bedroom has a king-sized bed with a bowed bonnet canopy, and there's a small balcony that looks out over the town through the inn's front columns.

Room 1 (low $200 range) is a large corner hideaway with a fireplace, a king-sized canopy bed, and a large deck under the trees. The spacious bathroom is equipped with its original fixtures, including a deep Roman-style tub and a shower stall.

Another romantic choice is room 7 (low $200 range), a rear corner room with parquet floors, a fireplace, a window seat, and a king-sized bed with a bonnet canopy. A covered deck is accessed through the small bathroom, which has a shower stall.

A clawfoot whirlpool tub, a marble shower, and a fireplace await behind the door of room 14 (mid $200 range), which is also furnished with a king-sized bed.

We weren't particularly impressed with rooms 5, 10, and 15.

THE MANSION INN

9 South Main Street
New Hope, PA 18938
Telephone: (215) 862-1231

Nine rooms, each with private bath; five with gas fireplaces;
two with tubs for two. Complimentary full breakfast served
at tables for two. Swimming pool. No handicapped access.
Smoking is not permitted. Two-night minimum stay required
during weekends; three-night minimum during holiday
periods. Expensive to deluxe.

Getting There
From Philadelphia on Interstate 95 north, take exit 31 to
Route 32 north into New Hope. Turn left at Bridge Street or
Route 179. The parking entrance to the inn is on the left.

THE MANSION INN   New Hope

We weren't looking for the Mansion Inn when our Bucks County tour drew us into the storybook village of New Hope. You might say the Mansion Inn found us. This creamy yellow-colored, Second Empire French Victorian–style manor is a traffic stopper and, as we discovered, a magnet for traveling romantics. Take our word for it: one look, and you'll want to stay the night.

When the home was built more than a century ago by a well-to-do livery merchant, New Hope was not much more than a rest stop on the road between Philadelphia and New York. The community later evolved into a well-known colony for artists, and it remains an artistic cultural center for the region. A number of shops and galleries and the Bucks County Playhouse are within walking distance. Before it became an inn in 1994, the structure served for years as a physician's office and hospital.

ROOMS FOR ROMANCE

In the Ashby Suite (low $200 range), the only room on the main floor, a delightful blue-and-white pattern is shared between the bed canopy and skirt, a Victorian love seat, a lamp shade, and the wall covering.

A favorite among honeymooners is the Windsor Suite (mid $200), which comprises half of the third floor. The sitting room, which offers a river view, has a fireplace, and the bedroom holds a king-sized canopy bed. In the bathroom is a two-person spa tub.

A spa tub for two with a shower attachment is hidden behind drapes in the corner of the Buckingham Room (high $100 range), which has its own outside entry. The queen-sized bed sits under white trusses. There's a sink in the room and a tiny toilet closet.

The Kensington Suite, one of the inn's most popular rooms, is found in the separate garden cottage at the rear of the property. Offering a private porch overlooking the garden, the suite has a window seat, a fireplace, a one-person spa tub, and a king-sized bed.

Nights at the Mansion Inn are made more comfortable thanks to ironed sheets, down comforters, and feather beds strewn with many pillows. If you can find the strength to pull yourselves out of bed in the morning, you'll find coffee and a newspaper at your door.

EVERMAY ON-THE-DELAWARE

River Road (P.O. Box 60)
Erwinna, PA 18920
Telephone: (610) 294-9100

Sixteen rooms, each with private bath. Complimentary
full or continental breakfast served at tables for two.
Restaurant. Handicapped access. Smoking is not
permitted. Two-night minimum stay required during
weekends; three-night minimum during holiday periods.
Moderate to expensive.

Getting There

From Philadelphia, follow Interstate 95 north to the New
Hope exit. Turn left at the bottom of the exit ramp and
follow signs to New Hope and Route 32 (River Road).
Drive north through New Hope, Lumberville, and Point
Pleasant. Evermay on-the-Delaware is five and a half
miles north of Point Pleasant.

EVERMAY ON-THE-DELAWARE ✍ Erwinna

Evermay's facade doesn't drip with Victorian ornamentation, the rooms aren't equipped with videocassette players, and the bathrooms don't have fancy marble or spa tubs for two. Evermay's low-key ambience and understated grace are the essence of its charm and romantic appeal. As Evermay's brochure says, "The hotel prides itself in providing both substance and style, with a lack of pretense."

A cozy nest for a romantic Bucks County weekend, this venerable country retreat has been around for better than two centuries. It still sits quietly by itself between the Delaware River and the Delaware Canal, surrounded by twenty-five acres of pastures, woodland, and gardens. Guests use the tow path for cross-country skiing, bicycling, and strolling. Two covered bridges are within walking distance.

The inn's dining room, which serves fixed-price six-course dinners Friday through Sunday ($60 range), is one of Bucks County's most highly rated restaurants.

ROOMS FOR ROMANCE

In the main inn, our favorite room is the Colonel William Erwin Room (upper $100 range), a spacious second-floor retreat with wide plank floors, an antique couch, and a river view.

Even the bathroom has a water view. The river can also be seen from the Pearl S. Buck Room (upper $100 range).

On the third floor, the Oscar Hammerstein Room (upper $100 range) boasts a river view from two windows. This room also has an antique bed with a matching marble-topped dressing table and two wing chairs. The bathroom has a shower stall.

The George Taylor Room (low $100 range) has a private bathroom that's detached from the room.

A separate two-story carriage house holds three rooms. Our recommended retreat here is the upstairs Redfield Suite (high $100 range). You can watch the river from the wood-trimmed clawfoot tub or from the queen-sized bed. A separate sitting room is furnished with a love seat and two chairs. The suite also has another bedroom, which makes it suitable for couples traveling together.

The M. J. Perelman (mid $100 range) is a self-contained cottage with a V-shaped ceiling and lots of windows. Furnishings include an antique bed, a dressing table, and a vintage settee. The step-up bathroom has a shower stall.

GLASBERN

2141 Packhouse Road
Fogelsville, PA 18051
Telephone: (610) 285-4723

Twenty-four rooms, each with private bath; ten with fireplaces;
seventeen with tubs for two. Complimentary full breakfast served
in restaurant. Swimming pool and restaurant. No handicapped
access. Smoking is not permitted. Two-night minimum stay
required during weekends and holiday periods. Moderate to
deluxe.

Getting There
From Interstate 78, take exit 14B north to Fogelsville. Turn left at
first light. Turn right at Church Street. Continue to Packhouse
Road and turn right. Inn is about one mile on the right.

GLASBERN   ❧   Fogelsville

Like a musician who crafts a wonderful song from the smallest seed of inspiration, innkeepers Beth and Al Granger created the expansive Glasbern compound from an abandoned antique German barn in the countryside near Allentown.

The skeletal remains of the old barn—hand-hewn beams and stacked stone walls—frame the impressive Great Hall, where guests check in, relax, and dine. Even the old farmer's ladders have been incorporated into the design. This romantically styled retreat, with its soaring ceiling, windows, and skylights, is Glasbern's focal point as well as its namesake. Glasbern means *glass barn* in Middle English.

The property also includes ponds, a swimming pool, and walking trails.

ROOMS FOR ROMANCE

Guest chambers are spread among the main inn and four other buildings. Three are located in a refurbished brick farmhouse. What used to be the home's kitchen is now room 22 (high $200 range), a very cozy, low-ceilinged retreat with a brick fireplace and a spa tub for two. A separate sunroom with slate floors holds a couch and a chair. The brick patio affords a nice local view.

The lower level unit in the Garden Cottage (around $300) has barn wood paneling and trusses, a heated slate floor, a wet bar, and a couch and chairs placed before a huge stone fireplace. The bedroom is up a few steps.

Carriage House rooms, rates for which run from around $200 to the mid $200 range, have woodburning fireplaces and spa tubs. In room 41, which overlooks the swimming pool, the spa sits in a sunroom area.

Four rooms at Glasbern are billed as "standard" accommodations. Offered in the mid $100 range, these have televisions and videocassette players, two cushioned chairs, in-room sinks, queen-sized beds, and bathrooms with tub-and-shower combinations.

CRESCENT LODGE AND COUNTRY INN

Route 191 Paradise Valley
Cresco, PA 18326
Telephone: (717) 595-7486; toll-free: (800) 329-9400

Thirty rooms, each with private bath; several with tubs for
two, videocassette players, and fireplaces. Swimming pool
and restaurant. No handicapped access. Smoking is allowed.
Two-night minimum stay required during weekends. Moderate
to deluxe.

Getting There
On Interstate 80 west near the New Jersey border, take exit 44
(Scotrun) to Route 611 north and then to Route 940 east. Follow
for four miles to Paradise Valley; inn is at the intersection of
Routes 191 and 940.

CRESCENT LODGE
AND COUNTRY INN ∞ Cresco

In an area with as many varied overnight options as the Poconos, picking the perfect spot isn't always easy, especially if you're first-time visitors armed only with the Sunday *New York Times* travel ads or a chamber of commerce lodging listing. Fortunately, we've done some sleuthing and identified a pair of Poconos destinations with definite romantic appeal.

Located in the aptly named Paradise Valley, Crescent Lodge and Country Inn is a venerable Poconos resort that's been in the same family for fifty years. Refurbished and enlarged over the years, the property also offers a popular restaurant as well as a lounge and a swimming pool.

ROOMS FOR ROMANCE

A number of rooms are offered in the main lodge, but for the most romantic experience, we prefer the cottages, each of which has a private sun deck. There are a number of different cottage options, with prices starting in the mid $100 range for a "deluxe room" with a canopied queen-sized bed.

Our favorite cottages are those with spa tubs for two. Rates for these are in the low to upper $200 range, and they are considerably lower in the spring and fall.

The prime accommodation here is a Mountain Jacuzzi (mid to upper $200 range), which enjoys a secluded mountain setting with pathway access to the central part of the property for those inclined to leave the cozy cottage. Inside is a queen-sized canopy bed, a kitchen, a balcony, a fireplace, and a sunken spa tub for the two of you. There's also a videocassette player.

A Jacuzzi Villa, a romantic hideaway without a kitchen, is available for about $30 less. These accommodations, some of which feature Southwestern decor, have king-sized beds, see-through fireplaces, videocassette players, and a sunken spa tub for two.

THE FRENCH MANOR

Huckleberry Road (P.O. Box 39)
South Sterling, PA 18460
Telephone: (717) 676-3244; toll-free: (800) 523-8200

Nine rooms, each with private bath; two with fireplaces;
two with tub for two. Complimentary full breakfast
served at tables for two or in your room. Restaurant.
Handicapped access. Smoking is allowed in the common
room. Two-night minimum stay required during
weekends. Expensive to deluxe.

Getting There
From Interstate 80 near the New Jersey border, take exit
52 and follow Route 447 north to Route 191. Drive north
to South Sterling. Turn left onto Huckleberry Road and
follow to inn.

THE FRENCH MANOR ❧ South Sterling

As the popularity of the Poconos Mountains has risen over the years, some of the region has suffered from overuse. Outlet stores, theme parks, and tacky souvenir shops compete for the attention of the millions of folks who visit each year. Thankfully, there are still some Poconos pockets, like South Sterling, where life remains slow and serene.

Mining executive Joseph Hirshhorn chose to build his opulent vacation chateau in this quiet corner of Huckleberry Mountain. Last occupied by department store mogul Samuel Kress, this grand residence-turned-inn was built by German and Italian master builders and artisans, who crafted the manor from local woods and fieldstone combined with imported material.

The on-site dining room serves elegant dinners most evenings. Jackets are required for men. Innkeepers Ron and Mary Kay Logan also operate the nearby Sterling Inn, whose indoor swimming pool and spa, small private lake, and tennis court are available to guests of the French Manor.

ROOMS FOR ROMANCE

The inn's most impressive accommodation is the Turret Suite (low $200 range). Occupying two levels of the stone-walled turret, the suite boasts windows on three sides offering a nice mountain view. One level is a living room; the bedroom is on the upper level.

Another romantic choice is the main-level Monte Carlo Room (high $100 range), whose walls and ceiling are paneled in dark cedar.

The secluded Carriage House, which has a more contemporary feel, offers two rooms and two suites. The Genevieve (low $200 range) is an opulent ground-floor suite with a king-sized bed with a massive, dark wood–framed canopy, a gas fireplace, a sitting area, and a raised corner spa tub for two. The separate bathroom has a shower.

The Geneva and San Remo Rooms in the Carriage House are offered in the mid $100 range.

CARNEGIE HOUSE

100 Cricklewood Drive
State College, PA 16803
Telephone: (814) 234-2424

Twenty-two rooms, each with private bath; twenty with
large soaking tubs. Complimentary continental breakfast
served at tables for two. Restaurant. Handicapped access.
Smoking is not permitted. Expensive to deluxe.

Getting There
From Interstate 80 take exit 23, Bellefonte. Follow signs
south to State College and Mount Nittany Expressway.
Take expressway to Toftrees exit. Turn right on Toftrees
Avenue. Inn is on the corner of Cricklewood Drive and
Toftrees Avenue.

CARNEGIE HOUSE ✍ State College

We hear about romantic destinations from a variety of sources: friends, colleagues, books, and magazines, as well as our own independent travels. We discovered Carnegie House through a letter to the editor published in a California newspaper. The writer, who had just returned from a Pennsylvania visit, was so ecstatic that we had to drop by State College for a look. You'll be glad we did.

The inn takes its name from the industrialist Andrew Carnegie, who once owned the land. The inn's lovely wooded location, overlooking a championship golf course in Toftrees Resort, was selected by Peter Schmid, who likened the setting to that of Greywalls, a Scottish inn set on the Muirfield golf course.

Peter, who has made a career in the hospitality industry, worked with the Toftrees developer to create the multipeaked, contemporary-style inn, whose warm interior carries a definite Scottish ambience. In fact, Carnegie House's motto, "Ceud Mile Failte," is an old Scottish phrase that means "one hundred thousand welcomes."

Carnegie House also has a restaurant that serves lunch and dinner. Guests receive a complimentary continental breakfast. Toftrees Resort has a swimming pool and tennis courts that are available to guests for a fee.

ROOMS FOR ROMANCE

Rooms at Carnegie House, which are priced from the mid $100 range to the mid $200 range, are clean and crisp, and are appointed with attractive draperies, thick carpeting, and traditional furniture. Woolen throws add an additional cozy touch. A number of rooms have king-sized beds with handsome partial canopies, and armoires conceal televisions and videocassette players. Bathrooms are spacious, and most have tubs for two. Some rooms have double beds.

For a romantic splurge, we suggest that you book one of the two suites on the third floor (high $200 range). These apartment-sized accommodations each have a wet bar, a powder room, a living room, and a bedroom.

New York

Daytime Diversions

Among the reasons we recommend the Lowell Hotel (see listing in this section) is its location within walking distance of Central Park and Manhattan museums as well as its easy access to shops ranging from funky to fashionable.

The beach at East Hampton, Long Island, is ranked by enthusiasts as one of America's best and cleanest.

Famed writer Washington Irving lived in Tarrytown, and his fairytale home, Sunnyside, is a popular stop on the Hudson Valley home tour circuit. So is Kykuit, the former Rockefeller family home, also in Tarrytown. In Westchester County, the Sugarloaf Art & Craft Village is a shopper's wonderland of cottage boutiques. Numerous wineries dot both sides of the Hudson River Valley.

Visitors to Lake Placid may choose from canoeing, swimming, downhill and cross-country skiing, golf, tennis, ice skating, and even bobsledding with an Olympic driver and brakeperson.

Tables for Two

Stroll the Upper East Side streets that surround our featured New York City destination, the Lowell, and you'll discover a number of charming neighborhood restaurants. The hotel also operates two popular on-site eateries. In East Hampton, two Main Street restaurants—Nick & Toni's and Della Femina—receive high marks.

In the Hudson River Valley, the Equus restaurant combines fine food with the enchanting and royal trappings of the Castle at Tarrytown. Le Petit Bistro in Rhinebeck is another recommended restaurant.

THE LOWELL HOTEL

28 East Sixty-third Street
New York, NY 10021
Telephone: (212) 838-1400; toll-free: (800) 221-4444

Sixty-five rooms, each with private bath; thirty-three
with fireplaces. Two restaurants. Limited handicapped
access. Smoking is allowed. Two-night minimum stay
required during weekends and holiday periods. Deluxe.

Getting There
The Lowell is on East Sixty-third Street between Park
and Madison Avenues.

THE LOWELL HOTEL   New York City

If your home base during a visit to New York City isn't important, you can easily find an anonymous hotel bargain in the Sunday *Times*. However, if the place you call home in the city is as important as shopping, dining, and the theater, the Lowell is an exceptional choice.

From the street, this European-style hostelry looks more like a townhouse than a hotel. In fact, it used to be a stylish residential hotel whose inhabitants included F. Scott and Zelda Fitzgerald and Noel Coward. Restyled as a hotel with only sixty-five suites and rooms, the Lowell consistently ranks among New York City's best small and sumptuous hotels.

Among the Lowell's many attributes is location. Hidden along a one-way street between Madison and Park Avenues on the Upper East Side, the hotel is within striking distance of the best of Manhattan. Broadway, Fifth Avenue shops, Central Park, and museums are within a healthy walk or a short cab ride away.

ROOMS FOR ROMANCE

Guest rooms at the Lowell are housed on seventeen floors. The majority have private kitchens and about half have fireplaces, wonderful carryovers from the apartment hotel days. Ten suites have private terraces.

All rooms have twice-daily maid service, multiline telephones, fax machines, video-cassette players, and caramel-colored Italian marble bathrooms with brass fixtures. All guests receive complimentary shoe shine and a morning newspaper delivered to their door. There is a fitness center on the second floor.

Deluxe rooms (high $400 range) have king-sized beds and dining tables for two. Eight of these have kitchens. In a Junior Suite (high $500 range), French doors divide the sitting area from the bedroom. Each has two televisions and a dining area for two.

We sampled room 14A ($600 range), a bright and spacious deluxe one-bedroom suite on the fourteenth floor. Delightful brick-floored double terraces, accented by plants and flower boxes and accessed through a French door, afford a sweeping lowrise view of much of the East Side.

The nicely windowed formal living room is furnished with rich draperies, chintz-covered chairs and a couch, as well as a writing desk. The kitchen is equipped with a stove, an oven, a dishwasher, and a refrigerator. There is also a separate dining area. The bedroom holds a king-sized bed with a partial canopy and a second television.

If you feel like splurging, the Hollywood Suite (around $900) on the thirteenth floor is a decadent specialty suite furnished with valuable movie memorabilia, a separate conference room, electronically controlled draperies, and an unbelievable wall-mounted audiovisual system. Another specialty suite is equipped with its own private gym.

MILL HOUSE INN

33 North Main Street
East Hampton, NY 11937
Telephone: (516) 324-9766

Eight rooms, each with private bath; six with gas
fireplaces; one with tub for two. Complimentary full
breakfast served at tables for four or in your room.
Handicapped access. Smoking is not permitted. Three-
night minimum stay required during in-season weekends
and four-night minimum stay required during holiday
periods. Deluxe.

Getting There
From Interstate 495 east on Long Island, take exit 70.
Turn right and follow road to Route 27 east. Continue
to the village of East Hampton. Follow past the light at
Newtown Lane, then bear left at North Main Street.
The inn is the fifth house on the left.

MILL HOUSE INN ❧ East Hampton

Because of the popularity of this seaside village, and because the two inns we admired are relatively small, we decided to share a pair of East Hampton getaway destinations. Combined, they still offer just over a dozen rooms, so make your plans early.

It was about one hundred years ago that this pleasing home was first remodeled and expanded, transformed from a traditional saltbox into the Dutch Colonial structure visitors encounter today.

Nearly a century later, Katherine and Dan Hartnett bought the place and waved their own magic wand, creating a lovely inn where guests are treated to such modern-day amenities as spa tubs and gas fireplaces. As part of the renovation, Katherine, formerly a chef at Manhattan's Pierre, installed a commercial kitchen, so be prepared for luscious breakfasts.

When not exploring the village, relaxing on the beach, or spending time in the privacy of their antique-furnished rooms, guests can be found on the front porch, which faces a historic windmill, or in the large backyard.

ROOMS FOR ROMANCE
Hampton Holiday (mid $300 range) is a very private third-floor room that's most often requested. It has a gas fireplace, a queen-sized bed, a dressing area, and a large bathroom with a spa tub for two.

Roses and lace are combined in the pretty decor of the Rose Room (around $300), another popular hideaway that has a queen-sized bed, a gas fireplace, and an antique armoire. The bathroom has a spa tub for one.

Hampton Breezes (low to mid $300 range) is a third-floor room that overlooks the backyard. Decorated in pink and green florals, the room has a queen-sized bed, a gas fireplace, and a bathroom with a soaking tub for one.

Hampton Classic (mid $200 range), on the first floor, faces Windmill Green across the street. This room has a shower, a queen-sized bed, and a twin bed.

Visitors should be aware that because of the inn's Main Street location, some traffic noise may be heard from the front-facing Patrick Lynch's Room and the Dominy Mill Room, especially during the busy summer months.

THE PINK HOUSE

26 James Lane
East Hampton, NY 11937
Telephone: (516) 324-3400

Six rooms, each with private bath; two with tubs for two.
Complimentary full breakfast served at communal table.
Swimming pool. No handicapped access. Smoking is not
permitted. Three-night minimum stay required during
weekend; four-night minimum during holiday periods.
Deluxe.

Getting There
From Interstate 495 on Long Island, take exit 70.
Follow Route 111 to Route 27 east, and continue to East
Hampton town pond. James Lane is the first right after
the pond.

THE PINK HOUSE ❦ East Hampton

Situated just across the street from the East Hampton town green, on Long Island, the Pink House is hard to miss. Just look for the pink house.

Built for a whaling captain in the mid-nineteenth century, the two-story home was refurbished and converted to a romantic getaway a few years ago by innkeeper Ron Steinhilber. The pale pink color was chosen by previous owners, and local rules state that the inn must remain this whimsical hue, which is actually quite pleasing.

One of East Hampton's most luxurious and charming getaway destinations, the Pink House is appointed with antique furnishings and art. The watercolors displayed throughout the home were painted by Ron's grandfather, Walter Steinhilber. The inn also has a swimming pool. During the warmer months, breakfast is served on the back porch overlooking the pool.

The shops and galleries at the center of East Hampton Village are about a fifteen-minute walk away. The East Hampton beach is known as one of the cleanest and nicest in the nation.

ROOMS FOR ROMANCE

A spa tub for two makes the Elk Room (upper $200 range) a favorite among traveling couples. This room sports a Southwestern motif. All rooms have private bathrooms, televisions, and telephones.

Another romantic favorite is the Blue Room (upper $200 range), whose bathroom is equipped with an oversized shower. In the bedroom is a cozy window seat and a queen-sized and partially draped pencil-post bed.

The single beds in the Twin Room can be joined to create a king-sized bed for two friendly people.

THE CASTLE AT TARRYTOWN

400 Benedict Avenue
Tarrytown, NY 10591
Telephone: (914) 631-1980

Thirty-one rooms, each with private bath; five with
fireplaces. Restaurant. Handicapped access. Smoking is
not permitted. Two-night minimum stay required during
weekends. Expensive to deluxe.

Getting There
From Route 119 west in Tarrytown, turn right on Benedict
Avenue. At second light turn left through the gate at 400
Benedict Avenue (opposite entrance to Hackley School).
Continue all the way up drive to the inn.

THE CASTLE AT TARRYTOWN ✍ Tarrytown

In our search for America's most romantic getaways, we've sampled hundreds of Victorians, contemporaries, Colonials, and Cape Cods. But nowhere had we found a genuine castle until we came upon the Castle at Tarrytown, an impressive landmark overlooking the Hudson River.

Journalist, playwright, and industrialist Howard Carroll commissioned this magnificent fortresslike home about a century ago, borrowing from castle designs in Ireland, Scotland, and Wales. Stonecutters, carpenters, and masons labored for several years to complete the building.

The wainscoting in the castle's Oak Room, which originally served as the family dining room, was moved from France, where it was part of a manor owned by Louis XIV. The Great Hall, with a forty-foot vaulted Gothic ceiling, stained-glass windows, and a musicians' balcony, can accommodate 150 guests for a seated meal.

The castle's restaurant, Equus, occupies elegantly furnished rooms, including the Oak Room. From the enclosed Garden Room, you can see the New York City skyline.

ROOMS FOR ROMANCE

Among the castle's royally appointed accommodations are five oversized suites that range in size from 750 to 900 square feet. The suites, which feature rich draperies and comfortable furnishings, all have Hudson River views, living rooms, working fireplaces, and elegant bathrooms.

Fit for a king and queen, the Caroline Suite (mid $400 range) is a romantic corner room furnished with a handsome canopied king-sized bed. At its foot sits a red love seat facing a decorative corner fireplace and windows with a view.

The centerpiece of the Contessa Suite (mid $400 range) is a canopied king-sized bed with a large carved panel headboard. There's also a romantic turret window seat.

If you have your heart set on spending a night in the castle's seven-story castle tower, ask for the Lismore Suite (about $600).

The castle also contains a smaller room (mid to upper $100 range) and a junior suite (upper $200 range).

In 1997, guest accommodations were expanded with the construction of a new wing containing two dozen new rooms. These rooms, painted a warm yellow and trimmed in cherry and mahogany woods, have beautifully dressed beds and sitting areas with sofas. Bathrooms feature white tile and marble-topped vanities. Deluxe rooms here (low to mid $200 range) have either two queen-sized beds or one king-sized bed.

INN AT LAKE JOSEPH

400 Saint Joseph Road
Forestburgh, NY 12777
Telephone: (914) 791-9506

Ten rooms, each with private bath; nine with fireplaces;
eight with tubs for two. Complimentary full breakfast
served at communal table, tables for two, or in your room.
Swimming pool and restaurant. No handicapped access.
Smoking is allowed except in dining areas. Two-night
minimum stay required during weekends; three-night
minimum during holiday periods. Expensive to deluxe.

Getting There
From the south, take Interstate 87 north, cross the Tappan
Zee Bridge and continue to exit 16. Take Route 17 west to
exit 104. Bear left to the light and turn left. Continue and
turn right on Route 42 south. Drive four and a half miles
and turn left at the inn's sign.

INN AT LAKE JOSEPH ✍ Forestburgh

Some years ago, when senior leaders of the Catholic Church desired solitary solace, they traveled to a hidden mountain refuge nestled within a dense forest fortress of the Catskills. Today, this lovely retreat is available to travelers pursuing not only peace and quiet but pleasures of the romantic kind.

The eclectic-style home was built around a century ago as a summer family home for a wealthy New York businessman, and it was later turned over to a group of Dominican nuns from Long Island who turned it into a religious retreat. In the thirties, Catholic Cardinals Spellman and Hayes used it as a vacation retreat, and it became known as the Cardinal House.

A charming country inn since the 1980s, the Inn at Lake Joseph is a self-contained destination offering comfortable lodgings, good food, and recreational activities. In addition to access to the 250-acre lake, the inn has a swimming pool and lawn games. Cross-country skiing, sleigh rides, and even horseback riding are offered during the winter. There's also a billiard room in the inn.

ROOMS FOR ROMANCE

The North Room (around $300) is a relatively new accommodation, and it's arguably the inn's most romantic. Located in the Carriage House, the North Room has a living room, a kitchenette, a working fireplace, a large whirlpool tub, and a spacious, private, raised and furnished veranda that overlooks the forest.

The South Room (around $300), also in the Carriage House, has a large living room with a couch and love seat, a dining table, a woodburning stove, and a cathedral ceiling.

In the same building is the East Room (around $300), a two-room suite with a fireplace and a spa tub.

The Red Room (mid $200 range), which is tastefully wallpapered in red and trimmed in white, is a nicely windowed room with two wing chairs, a canopied queen-sized bed, and a working fireplace. There's a spa tub in the bathroom.

One of the inn's choicest retreats is the Quiet Room (mid $200 range), where a comfy easy chair and ottoman are pulled close to a warming wood stove; a wood-framed spa tub for two beckons from a small alcove beneath twin windows. A nice view is offered from the four-poster king-sized bed.

OLD DROVERS INN

Old Route 22 (P.O. Box 100)
Dover Plains, NY 12522
Telephone: (914) 832-9311

Four rooms, each with private bath; three with fireplaces.
Dinner for two included in rates; complimentary full
breakfast served at tables for two or in your room.
A continental breakfast is served midweek. Restaurant.
No handicapped access. Smoking is allowed. Two-night
minimum stay required during weekends and holidays.
Deluxe.

Getting There
From Interstate 84 near the Connecticut border, take
Route 22 north. Or, if coming from the south, Interstate
684 north becomes Route 22 north after Brewster. The
inn is just off Route 22 between Wingdale and Dover
Plains.

OLD DROVERS INN ❧ Dover Plains

In the old days, professional New England cowboys, called drovers, rested up at this hospitable inn as they moved their cattle from the Harlem Valley to market in New York City. In one sense, not much has changed about the place over the years.

Only three families have occupied the property since the inn's construction in 1750, and each has obviously treated the structure with great care and respect. For example, the authentic and intriguing "tap room" still boasts the old stone walls and heavy wooden beams. The Federal Room, which once served as a restaurant, still has the wall murals that were hand-painted a half century ago.

It's doubtful, however, that the cattle drovers who once cooled their heels here would recognize the guest rooms that greet today's visitors. The original plank floors may still warp and creak with age, but today's guest accommodations far surpass those of the inn's early years. All rates include dinner for two and a full breakfast.

ROOMS FOR ROMANCE

Arguably the best room in the inn is the Meeting Room (around $400), which boasts an unusual curved ceiling. In this romantic hideaway, a woodburning fireplace is framed by two small windows and two comfortable chintz-covered chairs. Hooked rugs cover the antique plank floors. The two of you will be close and cozy in one of the two double beds here. The modest but modern bathroom has a tub-and-shower combination.

The nicely windowed and draped Sleigh Room (mid $300) is furnished with a beautiful antique queen-sized sleigh bed and a woodburning fireplace. The bathroom has a tub-and-shower combination.

The Cherry Room (mid to upper $300 range) is a bright room with matching cherry double beds and a woodburning fireplace. The bathroom has a tub-and-shower combination.

TROUTBECK

Leedsville Road

Amenia, NY 12501

Telephone: (914) 373-9681

Forty-two rooms, thirty-seven with private bath; several with fireplaces and tubs for two. Complimentary full breakfast served at tables for two or continental breakfast served in your room. Dinner is also included in rates. Swimming pool. Handicapped access. Smoking is allowed except in dining rooms. Two-night minimum stay required during weekends; two- to three-night minimum during holiday periods. Deluxe.

Getting There

From the south, take Interstate 684 north to Brewster. Continue beyond Brewster when Route 684 becomes Route 22. Follow Route 22 to Amenia. Turn right on Route 343. Continue for two and a half miles to inn's sign on the right. Turn right beyond the sign onto Route 2. After the bridge, the inn is the first driveway on the right.

TROUTBECK   Amenia

Because Troutbeck is essentially a corporate retreat during the work week, the first encounter many guests have with the estate isn't necessarily romantic. But when the weekends roll around, the working professionals put away their calculators and cell phones and return with their spouses or significant others for activities of a more intimate sort.

In its early years, the beautiful Tudor-style manor was the home of poet and naturalist Myron Benton, a friend of Ralph Waldo Emerson and Henry Thoreau. Later, poet and philosopher Joel Spingarn lived here, hosting such luminaries as Sinclair Lewis and Theodore Roosevelt. Black leaders conceived the NAACP at Troutbeck.

A self-contained resort, Troutbeck pampers guests with indoor and outdoor swimming pools, tennis courts, a fitness room, and a whirlpool and sauna. Depending on the time of your visit, you may try your hand at fishing or step into a pair of cross-country skis.

Rates include use of the facilities, breakfast and dinner, and an open bar with house wines and liquor drinks. Plan on spending between around $650 and $1,050 for a two-night stay. Many of the most romantic rooms carry a two-night minimum, especially in the winter months. Some rooms are available for one night during the summer.

ROOMS FOR ROMANCE

The main house, with its historic charm and elegance, is a good choice for a romantic getaway. Troutbeck Room One (high $800 range for two nights; around $500 for one night) has a queen-sized canopy bed, a sitting area, a porch, and a woodburning fireplace with a raised hearth.

Six sumptuous "great rooms" offering sofas, garden views, and spa tubs for two were added recently. The nicest of these is Great Room One (low $1,000 range for two nights; around $600 for one night), which often is used as a bridal suite. The wrought-iron king-sized bed is draped with mosquito netting, and there's a spa tub for two in the bathroom.

Several rooms are found in the Century Farm House, a separate building that's a combination of a 250-year-old building and a newer addition. Four of the newer rooms here (mid to upper $700 for two nights) have fireplaces; two of these have porches. Some of the bathrooms in the older section are shared.

Five more contemporary-styled guest accommodations are contained in the Garden House. Two of the rooms have fireplaces and garden-view decks.

LAKEHOUSE ON GOLDEN POND
Shelley Hill Road
Stanfordville, NY 12581
Telephone: (914) 266-8093

Nine rooms, each with private bath; seven with
fireplaces; seven with tubs for two. Complimentary
full breakfast served in the dining area or in your room.
No handicapped access. Smoking is not permitted.
Two-night minimum stay required during weekends
and holiday periods. Deluxe.

Getting There
From Taconia State Parkway–Rhinebeck, take Route 199
exit. Continue east on 199 and turn right on Route 53.
Drive three and a half miles and turn right on Shelley
Hill Road. Continue one mile and turn right into inn's
driveway.

LAKEHOUSE ON GOLDEN
POND   ✍   Stanfordville

There's no sign to identify the inn, so you'll need to be attentive to find this cedar-sided hideaway on your first pass. As we have frequently discovered, some of the most romantic destinations are the most out of the way.

The inn's name is romantic enough, but it's actually a bit deceiving. The main building is a spacious and contemporary structure that sits adjacent to what to us seems more like a small lake than a pond. The lake is part of the inn's private twenty-two-acre estate, and guests are welcome to explore the waters in the Lakehouse's fleet of paddle- and rowboats.

ROOMS FOR ROMANCE

All rooms have televisions, video-cassette players (there's a movie library on site), cassette and compact disc players, and minirefrigerators. Among the five rooms in the main inn building is the Master Suite (around $500), a corner room with loads of windows and a lake view. The king-sized bed, a work of art itself, has a carved wood canopy whose posts are draped with lace. There's also a sitting area with two leather chairs and an antique hobby horse.

A whimsical favorite is the Hunt Room (mid $300 range), which boasts a fox hunt motif. A collection of dolls is even dressed for a hunt. This room has a small sitting area with a table and chairs and a private deck with a wooded view. The bathroom has a spa tub for two and separate shower.

The largest and most expensive room in the inn, the Casa Blanca Suite (low $500 range), has a spa tub that's situated in the bedroom and surrounded by windows offering a lake view. It has a vaulted ceiling, a fireplace, a sofa, a dining area, and a lake-view deck.

Across the lake is the remote Boat House, which houses the Lakeside Quarters (low $400 range) and the Cliffside Quarters (low $300 range). Lakeside is a lovely lake-view room with a king-sized bed, a table and chairs, and a private deck that looks into the treetops. Cliffside Quarters is an attractive, wood-paneled room with a corner fireplace, a wooded view, and a small deck that does not offer complete privacy.

MANSAKENNING CARRIAGE HOUSE

29 Ackert Hook Road
Rhinebeck, NY 12572
Telephone: (914) 876-3500

Five rooms, each with private bath and fireplace; three
with tubs for two. Complimentary full breakfast served
in your room. Handicapped access. Smoking is allowed
on balconies and decks only. Two-night minimum stay
required during weekends; three-night minimum during
holiday periods. Deluxe.

Getting There
From the south, take Taconic Parkway north to the Pine
Plains/Red Hook exit (Rhinebeck). Drive west on Route
199, bearing left at Route 308. Turn left on Route 9,
follow for one mile, then turn left on Ackert Hook Road.
Continue one-half mile to inn's sign on the right. The inn
is on a private dirt drive on the left side.

MANSAKENNING CARRIAGE HOUSE ❧ Rhinebeck

We've all spent the night in "friendly" country inns whose well-meaning proprietors were a bit too friendly. If you are a pair of romantic travelers whose main getaway motivation is to get reacquainted with each other, this is your place. As innkeeper Michelle Dremann says, "Privacy and independence are a main part of our focus here."

Some accommodations have private entries and their own terraces for spending private time together outdoors, all have minirefrigerators, and a full breakfast is brought to your room in a basket—no awkward chitchat at a communal table for twelve. Even a weather report is delivered to your door. Carriage rides can also be arranged for the two of you.

Listed on the National Register of Historic Places, the Mansakenning is a hundred-year-old colonial home surrounded by five wooded and landscaped acres. The grounds include a koi pond, outdoor sitting areas, and outdoor game areas. The inn is located about one mile from Rhinebeck, a picturesque village nestled in the Hudson River Valley hills.

ROOMS FOR ROMANCE

In the main house, the Mansakenning Suite (mid $300 range) has a full list of romantic amenities: eleven windows with woodsy views, a king-sized bed, French doors opening to a wraparound balcony, a brick fireplace, and an oversized tile shower. It also has a private entry and separate driveway.

Four rooms are housed in the estate's converted carriage house. The Fox Den (high $300 range) is a bi-level suite on the second floor, and it features a cathedral ceiling, a king-sized canopy bed, a woodburning fireplace, and a sitting area. A private deck overlooks the grounds. A spa tub for two awaits in the skylit bathroom.

A rustic equestrian atmosphere prevails in the Saddlery (mid $300 range), a ground-floor carriage house room where saddles, bridles, and carriages were once stored. In the bedroom is a queen-sized bed with a wedding veil canopy, and there's a fireplace that can be seen from both the bed and the sitting room. The bathroom has a shower.

Country Covert (high $300 range) occupies much of the first floor of the carriage house, where horses were once stabled. The bedroom has a woodburning fireplace, and there's a cozy sitting room with a Victorian trundle bed. The bathroom has a spa tub. There's a private entry and a sitting area with a wooded meadow view. If the horses could only see their former stable now.

OLD CHATHAM SHEEPHERDING COMPANY INN

99 Shaker Museum Road
Old Chatham, NY 12136
Telephone: (518) 794-9774

Nine rooms, each with private bath; four with fireplaces; one
with tub for two. Complimentary full breakfast served at tables
for two. Restaurant. Handicapped access. Smoking is not
permitted. Two-night minimum stay required during weekends; three-night minimum during holiday periods. Deluxe.

Getting There

From intersection of Interstate 90 west and the Taconic
Parkway, take Highway 295 east to East Chatham. Turn left at
sign for Old Chatham and follow Albany turnpike three miles
to center of Old Chatham. Turn left on Route 13 and follow
for one mile to Shaker Museum Road. Turn right and continue
one-half mile to inn on the left.

OLD CHATHAM SHEEPHERDING COMPANY INN ✑ Old Chatham

The Hudson River Valley, the Berkshires, Saratoga—so many choices, so little time. Our recommendation is to sample all three—and more—by settling in at the Old Chatham Sheepherding Company Inn.

This romantic and strategically situated inn is just a short drive from the Hudson River, and the heart of the Berkshires is a twenty-minute car ride away. And if you'd rather not spend your time driving, the inn's expansive property offers swimming and innertubing on Kinderhook Creek, walking paths, and restful surroundings.

The two-hundred-year-old Georgian Colonial–style inn was the home of the late John Williams, a famed collector of Shaker artifacts. His impressive collection is housed in a museum across the street.

The establishment, which also boasts an outstanding on-site restaurant using farm-fresh ingredients, takes its name from the adjacent sheep farm operated by the innkeepers. It's reportedly the largest sheep dairy in the country.

ROOMS FOR ROMANCE

The wicker-furnished porch of the Suffolk Room (low $200 range) offers views of the gardens and the meadows beyond. This room has a beautiful queen-sized four-poster bed and a working fireplace, and the bathroom, tiled in white, has a two-headed shower big enough for the two of you.

Hampshire (mid $200 range), a small, two-room suite perfect for lovers seeking solitude, is located in the inn's cottage. It has a small sitting area and a cozy, romantic bedroom with a queen-sized bed. The tiled bathroom has a spa tub for one. A private deck affords sweeping views of the picturesque dairy farm down the road.

The inn's largest and most luxurious accommodation is Cotswold (low $300 range), whimsically decorated with a kayak, a deer head, and snowshoes, and appointed with a queen-sized four-poster bed and working fireplace. This room has a vaulted ceiling and hardwood floors, as well as a step-down bathroom with a shower and a large soaking tub. There's also a loft with two twin-sized trundle beds. French doors open to a furnished deck that has countryside views.

Located in a restored carriage house, Montadale (high $300 range) is a new split level suite whose upstairs bedroom has a four-poster bed and a tiled bathroom. Downstairs is a cozy sitting area with a stone fireplace and garden views through French doors.

THE LAMPLIGHT INN

231 Lake Avenue (P.O. Box 70)
Lake Luzerne, NY 12846
Telephone: (518) 696-5294; toll-free: (800) 262-4668

Seventeen rooms, each with private bath; twelve with
fireplaces; four with tubs for two. Complimentary full
breakfast served at tables for two. Handicapped access.
Smoking is not permitted. Two-night minimum stay
required during weekends; three-night minimum during
holiday periods. Moderate to expensive.

Getting There
Take Interstate 87 north to exit 21 Lake George–Lake
Luzerne. Follow Route 9N south for eleven miles. The
inn is on the right.

THE LAMPLIGHT INN ✍ Lake Luzerne

If history is any indication of an inn's romantic appeal, the Lamplight Inn is a winner. The colorful life of this Adirondack gem is steeped in romance.

It was built by a wealthy turn-of-the-century playboy lumberman who used the Victorian Gothic home as his summer funhouse. About one hundred years after its construction, sweethearts Gene and Linda Merlino bought the tired and neglected manor while they were dating. A few months later the two were married, and they spent their honemoon sprucing the place up for guests. And in the decade or so since, the inn has seen its share of passion, or so the guestroom diaries suggest.

If the inn's ten-acre property isn't sufficient to keep the two of you entertained, Lake George is within a ten-minute drive, and quaint Saratoga Springs is less than twenty miles away.

ROOMS FOR ROMANCE

The majority of rooms are found in the main inn. One of our favorites is the Victoria Room (mid $100 range), a nicely wallpapered room whose queen-sized bed has a dark wood-framed canopy. Within view of the bed is a brick gas fireplace.

Another romantic favorite is the Rose Room (mid $100 range), which was the original owner's master bedroom. This spacious and sunny front corner has a gas fireplace with a carved oak mantle.

Guests planning a romantic getaway should be aware that the private bathrooms of the Canopy and Wildflower Rooms are located across the hall from their respective quarters.

There are five suites (mid $100 range) in the Carriage House. The Saratoga, French Mountain, Woodside Romance, and White Birch Suites have queen-sized beds, spa tubs for two in the bedrooms, gas fireplaces, and baths equipped with tub-and-shower combinations. The Northern Exposure Suite has a shower for two, as well as a gas fireplace. All except the Saratoga Suite have private outdoor porches.

The Brookside Guest House, originally the caretaker's residence, sits next to a brook whose source is Lake Luzerne across the street. There are two rooms here, and each has a queen-sized bed, a gas fireplace, and a private bath with a tub-and-shower combination.

FRIENDS LAKE INN

Friends Lake Road
Chestertown, NY 12817
Telephone: (518) 494-4751

Sixteen rooms, each with private bath; five with tubs for
two; two with fireplaces. Complimentary full breakfast
served at tables for two or in your room. Restaurant. No
handicapped access. Smoking is not permitted, except in
bar area. Two-night miminum stay required during
weekends. Expensive to deluxe.

Getting There
Take Interstate 87 north to exit 23 and take Route 9
north. Continue through Warrensburg and turn onto
Route 28. Drive approximately five miles to Friends Lake
Road. Turn right and follow to the inn four and a half
miles down the road on the left.

FRIENDS LAKE INN ❧ Chestertown

After a weekend at Friends Lake Inn, we'll wager the two of you will leave as much more than friends. This charming small inn is designed and operated to fan the flames and stir the heart.

The oldest part of the building, dating from around 1850, was a farmhouse that was expanded later to become a boardinghouse serving workers at local tanneries. These days, innkeepers Greg and Sharon Taylor cater more to active couples attracted by such diversions as whitewater rafting on the Hudson River and snow skiing, as well as to those who desire nothing more than to lounge lazily on the shore of Friends Lake, which is just across the road and down the lane.

In 1996, Greg and Sharon, both wine aficionados, opened an attractive wine cellar dining room. The cellar holds more than ten thousand bottles. Their pairings of food and wine have earned praise from critics around the country. Happily, all room rates below include dinner for two.

ROOMS FOR ROMANCE

For the most romantic experience, we recommend rooms with lake views and/or spa tubs for two.

Room 11 (low $200 range), a second-floor deluxe junior suite with pine paneled walls, a cathedral ceiling, a river rock fireplace, a queen-sized bed, and a spacious window seat, won a national interior design award.

Rooms 12, 15, and 16 are the other second-floor deluxe junior suites offering lake-view window seats. These rooms carry similar rates.

On the third floor, rooms 14 and 17 (mid $200 range) boast spa tubs for two set against lake-view windows.

For travelers on a budget, rooms 8 and 10 on the first floor are traditional accommodations with lake views. These are offered in the high $100 range.

LAKE PLACID LODGE

P.O. Box 550 (Whiteface Inn Road)
Lake Placid, NY 12946
Telephone: (518) 523-2700

Thirty-seven rooms and cabins, each with private bath;
thirty-three with fireplaces; nineteen with tubs for two.
Complimentary full breakfast served in the dining room.
Continental breakfast can be delivered to your room.
Limited handicapped access. Smoking is not permitted.
Two-night minimum stay required during weekends; three-
night minimum during major holiday periods. Deluxe.

Getting There
Take Interstate 87 north to exit 30 (Lake Placid), and
follow Route 73 north. Continue to Route 86 west through
Lake Placid village. Turn right on Whiteface Inn Road at
the top of the hill. Follow for one and a half miles to Lake
Placid Lodge sign. Turn right to the lodge.

LAKE PLACID LODGE ❧ Lake Placid

If you're planning a trip to the Adirondack Mountains, be forewarned. Visiting Lake Placid without spending a night or two at this wonderfully restored lakeside lodge is like getting married and not taking a honeymoon.

Lake Placid Lodge has nestled on this high bank for over a half century. A careful refurbishment and upgrading preserved the rustic ambience while infusing the guest rooms with contemporary furnishings and modern-day conveniences. Blending Adirondack antiques with overstuffed chairs, and weathered log trusses with deep soaking tubs for two, the lodge represents an ideal romantic balance of yesterday and today.

Diversions at the lodge include canoes and paddleboats for lake explorations, fishing, hiking, a sandy swimming area, sight-seeing cruises aboard a tour barge, and an on-site restaurant. Downhill skiers may sample nearby Whiteface Mountain, and the Lake Placid Nordic Center, which is located adjacent to the lodge on Whiteface Club Golf Course, has miles of groomed ski and skating tracks. Indoor and outdoor ice skating arenas are located in the village of Lake Placid.

ROOMS FOR ROMANCE

Ah, where to begin. We'll start with the upper level of the main lodge, where the Whiteface Suite (around $500) boasts a large bedroom with a fireplace, a king-sized bed, a private lake-view deck, a sitting room, and a bathroom with a large soaking tub offering a lake and mountain view.

In the luxurious Hearthside ($300 to $400 range), a king-sized bed faces a massive stone fireplace with a built-in bookcase. Two comfortable chairs flank the fireplace. In the bathroom is a large soaking tub and a separate shower for two. This room, which features paneling, log trusses, and Indian prints, has a wooded view.

Located in a separate lodge, the Birch Room (around $500) is paneled in rough-cut cedar and appointed with birch furnishings. The room has his-and-her bathrooms (with double shower and double soaking tub), a fireplace, and a large private porch.

In 1996, the lodge added a collection of fifteen rustic cabins adjacent to the property, all located just inches or feet away from Lake Placid and all offering sweeping views of the mountains. Renovated with Adirondack appointments and twig detailing, the cabins just might be the property's most romantic accommodations. All have large stone fireplaces and beautiful bathrooms with deep soaking tubs for two and separate showers with double heads. You can choose from spacious studio cabins with open-beamed ceilings and huge picture windows; one-bedroom, one-bath cabins with large sitting rooms and bedrooms; and two-bedroom, two-bath cabins. All have wet bars, and room service is available. Rates run from the low $400 range to the mid $600 range.

BELHURST CASTLE

Route 14 South (P.O. Box 609)

Geneva, NY 14456

Telephone: (315) 781-0201

Thirteen rooms, each with private bath; four with
fireplaces; one with tub for two. Complimentary
continental breakfast served in the restaurant or
in your room. No handicapped access. Smoking is
allowed. Moderate to deluxe.

Getting There

Take the New York State Thruway (Interstate 90)
to exit 42, and take Route 14 south. The inn is eight
and a half miles from the thruway exit.

BELHURST CASTLE ❧ Geneva

Boasting castlelike stone turrets, tiny dormers, and multiple chimneys, this intriguing home was commissioned by a millionaire in the early 1800s and built from materials primarily imported from Europe. Before becoming an inn, Belhurst Castle operated as a gambling casino.

Centrally located for explorations of the Finger Lakes Region, Belhurst Castle occupies a romantic setting adjacent to Seneca Lake. Rochester, Syracuse, and Corning are within one hour of the inn, and Finger Lakes wineries are an easy drive away.

The castle has a lake-view restaurant that serves lunch and dinner and Sunday brunch. Among the many unusual features of the inn is a small spigot protruding from a piece of marble on the second-floor landing. The spigot dispenses complimentary New York chablis, and it's available to guests round the clock.

ROOMS FOR ROMANCE

Most couples set their sights on the romantic stone turret that houses the luxurious Tower Suite (around $300). Here you'll be treated to a sitting room with a sofa, a bedroom with a queen-sized bed, and a large bathroom with a spa tub for two.

If you enjoy the outdoors, we recommend Maureen's Room (around $200), which has a private balcony with a lake view. Inside is a queen-sized canopy bed and a full tiled bathroom.

The Dwyer Suite (mid $200 range) offers a full lake view, beautiful stained-glass windows, a dining alcove, a sitting area with a sofa, a queen-sized four-poster bed, and a fireplace.

The Ice House (low $100 range), located on the grounds behind the castle, has a cozy loft bedroom reached by a spiral staircase.

MORE TRAVEL RESOURCES
FOR INCURABLE ROMANTICS

Weekends for Two in New England: 50 Romantic Getaways

Weekends for Two in Northern California: 50 Romantic Getaways (Revised and Updated)

More Weekends for Two in Northern California: 50 All-New Romantic Getaways

Weekends for Two in Southern California: 50 Romantic Getaways (Revised and Updated)

Weekends for Two in the Pacific Northwest: 50 Romantic Getaways (Revised and Updated)

Weekends for Two in the Southwest: 50 Romantic Getaways

Each illustrated with more than 150 color photos, these books by Bill Gleeson are the definitive travel guides to the nation's most romantic destinations.

FREE TRAVEL UPDATES

We continue to discover new romantic destinations and reevaluate our currently featured inns and small hotels, and we're happy to share this information with readers. For a free update on our new discoveries, recommendations, and new books in the *Weekends for Two* series, visit the Chronicle Books Web Site at www.chroniclebooks.com or send a stamped, self-addressed business-sized envelope to Bill Gleeson, Weekends for Two Update, P. O. Box 6324, Folsom, CA 95763. We also appreciate hearing about your own romantic discoveries as well!

CAST YOUR VOTE

The Mid-Atlantic's Most Romantic Hotel or Inn

Complete and mail to Bill Gleeson, Weekends for Two, P.O. Box 6324, Folsom, CA 95763. Please enclose a self-addressed stamped envelope if you'd like a response or a free travel update.

Our favorite romantic retreat in the Mid-Atlantic
(doesn't have to be featured in this book):

_____
Name of hotel/inn

_____
City/Town/State

What makes this place special:

_____

_____

Signed (names/addresses are not for publication):

_____
I have no connection with the operators of this property.

INDEX